COLLABORATIVE TEAMS THAT *Transform* SCHOOLS

THE NEXT STEP IN PLCS

Robert J. Marzano • Tammy Heflebower
Jan K. Hoegh • Philip B. Warrick • Gavin Grift

with
Laurel Hecker
Janelle Wills

MARZANO
—Research—

555 North Morton Street
Bloomington, IN 47404
888.849.0851
FAX: 866.801.1477

email: info@marzanoresearch.com
marzanoresearch.com

Visit **marzanoresearch.com/reproducibles** to download the reproducibles in this book.

Printed in the United States of America

Library of Congress Control Number: 2015918490

ISBN: 978-1-943360-03-1

Text and Cover Designer: Rian Anderson

Marzano Research Development Team

Director of Content & Resources
Julia A. Simms

Editorial Manager
Laurel Hecker

Production Editor
Ming Lee Newcomb

Editorial Assistants / Staff Writers
Elizabeth A. Bearden
Christopher Dodson

Marzano Research Associates

Mario Acosta
Tina H. Boogren
Bev Clemens
Sally Corey
Jane Doty Fischer
Jeff Flygare
Jason E. Harlacher
Tammy Heflebower
Lynne Herr
Mitzi Hoback
Jan K. Hoegh
Jeanie Iberlin
Russell Jenson

Bettina Kates
Jessica McIntyre
Diane E. Paynter
Kristin Poage
Cameron Rains
Tom Roy
Mike Ruyle
Julia A. Simms
Gerry Varty
Philip B. Warrick
Kenneth C. Williams
David C. Yanoski

Table of Contents

Reproducible pages are in italics.

About the Authors

Robert J. Marzano, PhD, is the cofounder and CEO of Marzano Research in Denver, Colorado. During his forty-eight years in the field of education, he has worked with educators as a speaker and trainer and has authored more than forty books and 250 articles on topics such as instruction, assessment, writing and implementing standards, cognition, effective leadership, and school intervention. His books include *The Art and Science of Teaching, Leaders of Learning, The Classroom Strategies Series, A Handbook for High Reliability Schools, Awaken the Learner,* and *Managing the Inner World of Teaching.* His practical translations of the most current research and theory into classroom strategies are known internationally and are widely practiced by both teachers and administrators. He received a bachelor's degree from Iona College in New York, a master's degree from Seattle University, and a doctorate from the University of Washington.

Tammy Heflebower, EdD, is a senior scholar at Marzano Research with experience working in urban, rural, and suburban districts throughout North America, Europe, and Australia. Tammy has served as an award-winning classroom teacher, building leader, district leader, regional professional development director, and national trainer. She has also been an adjunct professor of curriculum, instruction, and assessment at several universities and a prominent member and leader of numerous state and national educational organizations. Tammy is an author of *Teaching & Assessing 21st Century Skills* and the award-winning *A School Leader's Guide to Standards-Based Grading,* as well as a contributor to over a dozen other publications. She holds a bachelor of arts from Hastings College, where she was honored as Outstanding Young Alumna and inducted into the athletic hall of fame. She has a master of arts from the University of Nebraska Omaha and a doctorate of education in educational administration and an educational administrative endorsement from the University of Nebraska–Lincoln.

Jan K. Hoegh is an associate vice president of Marzano Research. She is a former classroom teacher, professional development specialist, assistant high school principal, and curriculum coordinator. Jan, who has thirty years of experience in education, also served as assistant director of statewide assessment for the Nebraska Department of Education, where her primary focus was Nebraska State Accountability test development. She has served on numerous statewide and national standards and assessment committees and has presented at national conferences. As an associate vice president of Marzano Research, Jan works with districts across the country, primarily focusing on high-quality classroom assessment practices, as they strive to improve student achievement. Her passion for education, combined with extensive knowledge of curriculum, instruction, and assessment provides credible support for teachers, leaders, schools, and districts. She is an author of the books *Using Common Core Standards to Enhance Classroom Instruction and Assessment* and the award-winning *A School Leader's Guide to Standards-Based Grading.* Jan holds a bachelor of arts in elementary education and a master of arts in educational administration, both from the University of Nebraska at Kearney. She also earned a specialization in assessment from the University of Nebraska–Lincoln.

Philip B. Warrick, EdD, is an associate vice president of Marzano Research and works with teachers and school leaders internationally. He was an award-winning administrator in Waverly, Nebraska, where he was selected as Nebraska Outstanding New Principal of the Year in 1998. In 2003, he was invited to attend the Gallup Corporation's Nebraska Educational Leadership Institute, and he was recognized as the Nebraska State High School Principal of the Year in 2005. Phil is a former regional president of the Nebraska Council of School Administrators (NCSA) and was appointed to the NCSA legislative committee, where he served as committee chair for one year. In 2008, he became campus principal at Round Rock High School in Round Rock, Texas, which serves approximately three thousand students. In 2010, Phil participated in the inaugural Texas Principals' Visioning Institute, where he worked with other principals to develop ideas and practices to help improve education for Texas students. He is a coauthor of *A School Leader's Guide To Standards-Based Grading* and *A Handbook for High Reliability Schools*, and a contributor to *Coaching Classroom Instruction.* He earned a bachelor of science from Chadron State College in Chadron, Nebraska and his master's and doctoral degrees from the University of Nebraska–Lincoln.

Gavin Grift is the executive director of Hawker Brownlow Professional Learning Services. He is the coauthor of numerous books and articles, including *Assessing the Whole Child, Teachers as Architects of Learning,* and *Transformative Talk.* With extensive experience as a teacher, assistant principal, and educational coach, Gavin's passion, commitment, and style have made him an in-demand presenter of keynotes, seminars, and in-school support days. As a speaker, he connects with national and international audiences on focus areas including professional learning communities, coaching, and quality teacher practice. Gavin has served as director for the Association of Innovation in Education and as curriculum hub leader for the Australian National Schools Network. He led the formation of a professional learning community network across Australia, culminating in the establishment of the Centre for Professional Learning Communities in 2015. Gavin also works as a training associate for Thinking Collaborative, where he served as global outreach consultant in 2013. Gavin holds a bachelor of education degree from Melbourne University in Victoria and a graduate diploma of education from Deakin University.

Laurel Hecker is an editorial manager for Marzano Research in Denver, Colorado and a coauthor of *Teaching Reasoning: Activities and Games for the Classroom.* Laurel's writing and editing experience extends across a range of topics and formats, including articles for the *Cipher* news magazine, website and social media content for local businesses, research reports, and creative pieces. She has also worked in outdoor education as a Girl Scout counselor and trip coordinator. She is a graduate of Colorado College, where she earned a bachelor of arts degree in English with a concentration in poetry writing.

 **Janelle Wills, PhD,** is the director of Marzano Institute Australia. Janelle is the lead training associate for High Reliability Schools, the Art and Science of Teaching, and other Marzano Research topics. She works extensively with schools, regions, and systems throughout Australia. With over thirty years of teaching and leadership experience, Janelle has a strong commitment to continued learning enabling her to remain both informed and innovative in her approaches. Through practical application, she has been able to link theory to practice, resulting in the development of significant initiatives both within and across schools at a sector level. Janelle has a strong belief in the importance of teaching as a profession and fervently promotes the need for teachers to actively engage with research through action research and reflective practice. Janelle holds bachelor's, master's, and doctoral degrees in education. Her doctoral degree focused on self-efficacy and contributed to the field of knowledge pertaining to special education, gifted education, assessment, and feedback.

About Marzano Research

Marzano Research is a joint venture between Solution Tree and Dr. Robert J. Marzano. Marzano Research combines Dr. Marzano's more than forty years of educational research with continuous action research in all major areas of schooling in order to provide effective and accessible instructional strategies, leadership strategies, and classroom assessment strategies that are always at the forefront of best practice. By providing such an all-inclusive research-into-practice resource center, Marzano Research provides teachers and principals with the tools they need to effect profound and immediate improvement in student achievement.

Introduction

The importance of collaboration in general has been prominent in the literature on education since at least the 1970s, and the concept of a *professional learning community* (PLC) in particular has been prevalent since at least the 1990s. The central theme of this book is that the PLC process is on the verge of a quantum leap in terms of its influence on the functioning of a school and, ultimately, its influence on student learning. This next step will take place by expanding the responsibilities of collaborative teams, enabling them to transform the scope and content of the curriculum, the nature and function of classroom assessments, the manner in which instruction is planned and executed, the system in which teachers develop, and the way schools are led. These proposed changes to curriculum, assessment, instruction, teacher development, and school leadership have been circulating for years but have never before been directly connected to the inner workings of a collaborative team and the interaction between collaborative teams. In effect, this book provides a picture of collaborative teams and the PLC process hitherto not seen—a picture we believe represents the long-term future of PLCs.

We begin with a brief but comprehensive review of the research and theory behind the PLC movement. Although you might be eager to move right into those chapters that provide practical recommendations for educators, we strongly encourage you to examine the research and theory, as it is the foundation for the book. Indeed, a basic purpose of *Collaborative Teams That Transform Schools* is to present the most useful strategies based on the strongest research and theory available.

Following our discussion of the historical and theoretical context of the PLC movement, chapter 2 explores the schoolwide and team-specific cultural foundations that support effective PLCs. Chapters 3 through 6 each present an area of education that can be transformed by collaborative teams: curriculum, assessment, instruction, and teacher development. Finally, chapter 7 considers the role of school leaders in supporting and advancing the PLC process.

How to Use This Book

Educators can use *Collaborative Teams That Transform Schools* as a self-study text that presents a complete model of effective PLCs. Each chapter explains steps and strategies educators can implement to enhance the PLC process. As you progress through the chapters, you will also encounter comprehension questions. It is important to complete these questions and compare your answers with those in appendix A (page 117). Such interaction provides a review of the content and allows a thorough examination of your understanding. When groups or teams of teachers or administrators use this book to examine the PLC process, team members should answer the questions independently and then compare their answers in small- or large-group settings. In addition, chapters 2 through 6 each include a self-evaluation survey. Collaborative teams can have their members complete these surveys to gauge their progress on the recommendations in each chapter.

CHAPTER 1 | Research and Theory

Of the many initiatives to pass through education, one of the most widely recognized is the concept of professional learning communities. Generally speaking, this term refers to a schoolwide system of teacher teams that collaborate on issues of instruction, assessment, and other school topics with the goal of improving student learning.

The most popular conception of PLCs is likely the one articulated by Richard DuFour and his colleagues (for example, DuFour & Eaker, 1998; DuFour, DuFour, & Eaker, 2008; DuFour, DuFour, Eaker, & Many, 2010). This model has a number of strong theoretical and research-based tenets, and its core component is a set of four critical questions that effective PLCs should address. As articulated by Richard DuFour and Robert Eaker, they are:

1. What is it we want our students to know?
2. How will we know if our students are learning?
3. How will we respond when students do not learn?
4. How will we enrich and extend the learning for students who are proficient?

DuFour and his colleagues have offered many diverse answers to these questions (for example, DuFour, DuFour, Eaker, & Many, 2010; DuFour, DuFour, Eaker, & Karhanek, 2010; DuFour & Fullan, 2013). In this book, we will approach the questions from a unique perspective. Specifically, we believe that these questions must be addressed simultaneously. The manner in which the first question is answered dramatically affects the way in which the second question is effectively answered, and so on.

In addition to providing a unique and internally cohesive answer to the four original questions, we add a fifth and a sixth.

5. How will we increase our instructional competence?
6. How will we coordinate our efforts as a school?

Table 1.1 (page 4) lists all six questions and the education area emphasized by each.

Table 1.1: The Six Questions and Their Emphases

Question	Area of Emphasis
What is it we want our students to know?	Curriculum
How will we know if our students are learning?	Assessment
How will we respond when students do not learn?	Instruction
How will we enrich and extend the learning for students who are proficient?	Instruction
How will we increase our instructional competence?	Teacher development
How will we coordinate our efforts as a school?	Leadership

As indicated in table 1.1, the first question (What is it we want our students to know?) is fundamentally a curriculum issue. The second question (How will we know if our students are learning?) is an assessment issue. The third question (How will we respond when students do not learn?) and fourth question (How will we enrich and extend the learning for students who are proficient?) are both instructional issues. The fifth question (How will we increase our instructional competence?) deals with teacher development. The sixth question (How will we coordinate our efforts as a school?) deals with leadership. These six questions not only offer a new perspective on the PLC process but can also serve as transformational forces when answered in specific ways. Before we consider these questions and their respective emphases, we first consider the historical and theoretical development of the PLC process.

The Nature of Organizations

Organizations, by definition, are made up of people and their interactions. Within an organization, no one truly acts independently; one's actions and behaviors affect—and are affected by—the actions and behaviors of other members of the organization. As Jeffrey Pfeffer and Robert I. Sutton (2000) put it, "Behavior and performance are influenced by the actions, attitudes, and behaviors of many others in the immediate environment" (p. 158). Organizational theorist Donald A. Schön (1983) described organizations as "repositories of cumulatively built-up knowledge: principles and maxims of practice, images of mission and identity, facts about the task environment, techniques of operation, stories of past experience which serve as exemplars for future action" (p. 242). In other words, organizations have the ability to store information.

However, a great deal of the organizational knowledge that develops over time cannot be stored formally—written procedures and other documents do not suffice to record practical or tacit knowledge (Pfeffer & Sutton, 2000). Instead, this information exists within the dynamics of the organization itself, "by the stories people tell to each other, by the trials and errors that occur as people develop knowledge and skill, by inexperienced people watching those more experienced, and by experienced people providing close and constant coaching to newcomers" (Pfeffer & Sutton, 2000, p. 19). In light of these ideas about the ways knowledge is shared within organizations, it seems rather intuitive that increased collaboration would lead to an increase in both organizational and individual knowledge.

Development Through Collaboration

The importance of collaboration as a method for professional improvement became evident in both the business and education sectors over the course of the 1970s and 1980s (Aram, Morgan, & Esbeck, 1971; de Geus, 1988; Levitt & March, 1988; Shrivastava, 1983). In a 1986 article in *Educational Leadership*, Shirley M. Hord summarized various theories regarding collaboration and identified ten essential features of effective collaboration; table 1.2 displays these ten features.

Table 1.2: Hord's Ten Features of Organizational Collaboration

Feature	Description
Needs and interests	"When gain is mutual and interest is sufficiently heightened, collaboration is possible."
Time	"The necessary time must be devoted to joint endeavors."
Energy	"Collaboration requires effort."
Communication	"The collaborating mode is a sharing one, and sharing is grounded in continuing communication."
Resources	"Collaborating organizations share funds, staff, and other resources."
Organizational factors	"While the organizations are the framework, the people within them do the actual work. Collaborating individuals within an organization promote similar activities between organizations."
Control	"When participants are willing to relinquish personal control and assume more risk, they create a more flexible environment and can move closer to collaboration."
Perceptions	"Taking the pulse or checking the perceptions of others involved contributes to the collaborating climate."
Leadership	"Strong leaders who express an enthusiastic, positive example of collaborating on many levels encourage overall collaboration in the organizations."
Personal traits	"'If there is any personality characteristic needed to function in the [collaborating] approach, it is probably simple patience' (Murray & Smith, 1974)."

Source: Adapted from Hord, 1986, p. 26.

The characteristics of organizational collaboration listed in table 1.2 clearly show that both structural and humanistic changes are required for organizations to operate collaboratively. Features such as time and resources must be redistributed to allow for collaboration. The individuals who make up the organization must buy into a common vision and be willing to devote energy to the cause, communicate with others, relinquish some personal control, and set positive examples for others. The identification of these key organizational traits sets the stage for the development of practical collaborative strategies.

The Many Faces of PLCs

The collective ideas about effective professional collaboration (see also Rosenholtz, 1991), along with those about reflective practice (Schön, 1983, 1987; Stenhouse, 1975), formed the foundation for the concept of professional learning communities. The term *professional learning community* became popular in education research and theory in the 1990s (Cuban, 1992; Hord, 1997; Louis, Kruse, & Associates, 1995; Louis, Marks, & Kruse, 1996; McLaughlin, 1993). Since then, the concept has evolved and grown through the work of its many notable proponents, including Milbrey W. McLaughlin, Joan E. Talbert, Judith Warren Little, Karen Seashore Louis, Jane B. Huffman, Kristine K. Hipp, Thomas Many, Robert Eaker, Rebecca DuFour, and Richard DuFour. Despite the many volumes that have been written on this topic, it can still be difficult to define.

Hord (1997) purported that a PLC engages teachers in a cycle of looking at what is happening in their school; determining if they can make it a better place by changing curriculum, instruction, or relationships between community members; and assessing the results—all with the goal of enhancing their effectiveness as professionals. Similarly, Louise Stoll, Ray Bolam, Agnes McMahon, Mike Wallace, and Sally Thomas (2006) stated that the term "suggests a group of people sharing and critically interrogating their practice in an ongoing, reflective, collaborative, inclusive, learning-oriented, growth-promoting way" (p. 223). Kathleen Fulton and Ted Britton (2011) identified the goal of a PLC as "focusing teachers on improving their practice and learning *together* about how to increase student learning" (p. 7). As mentioned previously, one of the best-known articulations of PLCs comes from DuFour, et al. (2008): "We define a professional learning community as *educators committed to working collaboratively in ongoing processes of collective inquiry and action research to achieve better results for the students they serve*" (p. 14).

These definitions all indicate that a PLC is an ongoing process. Teachers and administrators within a PLC are expected to become learners themselves, using research from the field and from within their own schools and classrooms to inform and adjust curriculum, instruction, and assessment. They also work together, sharing resources and knowledge to help one another improve their teaching practices. All of this is done with the primary goal of increasing student learning—success is not measured by what or how teachers teach, but by how much students learn.

Building on these general definitions, researchers and theorists have identified specific characteristics of effective PLCs. A summary of some of these characteristics is displayed in table 1.3. Taken together, the myriad definitions and descriptions emphasize collaboration, critical inquiry, and improving student learning. Few educators would deny that these notions seem like good ideas—which begs the question, Why haven't PLCs been more widely and effectively implemented as tools for school reform?

Issues With Implementation

One of the major problems hindering successful PLC implementation is a lack of clarity about the concept. Though broad definitions abound, the term is not standardized and often lacks practical, specific guidelines for development. As DuFour (2004) described:

> The idea of improving schools by developing *professional learning communities* is currently in vogue. People use this term to describe every imaginable combination of individuals with an interest in education—a grade-level teaching team, a school committee, a high school department, an entire school district, a state department of education, a national professional organization, and so on. In fact, the term has been used so ubiquitously that it is in danger of losing all meaning. (p. 6)

In the late 1990s and early 2000s, the PLC concept became widely known over a short period of time, and "rapid diffusion led also to ambiguity" (Louis, 2006, p. 479). While the ideals and aims of the PLC concept gained popularity, there were few specific instructions for *how* to establish a productive PLC. This made it

Table 1.3: Characteristics of Effective PLCs

Characteristic	Supporting Studies
Mutual support and trust among teachers	Bolam, McMahon, Stoll, Thomas, & Wallace, 2005 Fulton & Britton, 2011 Hord, 2009
Shared vision and values	Bolam et al., 2005 Fulton & Britton, 2011 Hord, 2009 Timperley, Wilson, Barrar, & Fung, 2007
Focus on improving student learning	Bolam et al., 2005 Fulton & Britton, 2011 Hord, 2009 Timperley et al., 2007
Focus on teacher growth and professional development	Annenberg Institute for School Reform (AISR), 2004 Bolam et al., 2005 Hord, 2009 Louis et al., 1995
Intentional and systematic support of the collaborative model	Bolam et al., 2005 Fulton & Britton, 2011 Hord, 2009 Louis et al., 1995 Morrissey, 2000 National Center for Literacy Education (NCLE), 2013
Inquiry-based approach and use of evidence	AISR, 2004 Fulton & Britton, 2011 NCLE, 2013 Timperley et al., 2007

inherently difficult for teachers, administrators, and other school staff to manifest the desirable vision of a PLC. Furthermore, most educators had not previously experienced a PLC and therefore could not draw upon prior knowledge. Even as the PLC concept has become more established, precise directions are often still lacking. Schools, departments, or groups of teachers attempting PLC work "may have vague plans that entail meeting together and working toward agreed-upon goals" (Mindich & Lieberman, 2012, p. 5), but without further specificity, good intentions often fail to produce results.

Inadequate guidance can also lead to the perception that the PLC concept is an easy fix that improves teacher and student learning, increasing the amount of time allotted for collaboration. Time for collaboration is, of course, one requirement of a successful PLC; however, "simply giving teachers time to talk [is] not enough to promote either their own learning or that of their students" (Timperley et al., 2007, p. 205). If a PLC is to effect change, collaborative efforts must be structured and purposeful. For example, one specific structure for PLCs is a set of conversational norms that encourage participants to "challenge problematic beliefs" and "test the efficacy of competing ideas" (Timperley et al., 2007, p. 203). Absent this and other conditions, collaborative time might simply reinforce the status quo (Timperley et al., 2007). Just as writing a set of academic standards does not ensure that all students will learn that material (DuFour, 2004), setting aside time for teachers and administrators to meet does not guarantee meaningful collaboration.

Another hindrance to wide PLC implementation is skepticism and resistance to change among staff:

> Despite compelling evidence indicating that working collaboratively represents best practice, teachers in many schools continue to work in isolation. Even in schools that endorse the idea of collaboration, the staff's willingness to collaborate often stops at the classroom door. (DuFour, 2004, p. 9)

The level of collaboration required in a PLC is a substantial change from the way most teachers have done their jobs in the past. Some teachers prefer working alone, viewing collaboration as a waste of time or an impediment to getting work done; others doubt that collaboration positively impacts student achievement (Elbousty & Bratt, 2010). Research disputes these opinions, however, showing that teamwork can have a significant positive impact.

Benefits of the PLC Process

Research on the topic of collaboration from fields such as cognition and expertise supports the most general and fundamental assumption of PLCs—that working together produces better results than working alone. Some theories of cognition posit that thinking and reasoning are most effective when distributed across a system or group, rather than confined to an individual (Putnam & Borko, 2000). Consider the example of a U.S. Navy ship (Hutchins, 1990, 1991): numerous crewmembers perform specific tasks, ultimately working together to complete work too complex for one person to do alone.

Collaboration also plays an important role in reflective practice. Reflective practice is an important pathway to expertise in education and other disciplines. It is also difficult to engage in reflective practice alone. Indeed, Schön (1983) stated, "The teacher's isolation in her classroom works against reflection-in-action. She needs to communicate her private puzzles and insights, to test them against the views of her peers" (p. 333). Collaborative problem solving is, in general, superior to problem solving in isolation simply because a group provides more perspectives on an issue. Interaction with others "expand[s] and test[s] the new concepts as part of the learning experience" (Morrissey, 2000, p. 4). A similar dynamic applies to growth and learning about oneself. Even extremely self-aware and critical people have blind spots, but input and feedback from others can help identify and improve them (Brookfield, 1995).

These more general benefits of collaboration are further supported by research on PLCs and collaboration in schools. In the following sections, we explore how the PLC process benefits teachers, students, and school leaders.

Benefits for Teachers

One of the most frequently proposed benefits of the PLC process is that it offers a more effective means of providing professional learning opportunities to teachers. As explained by V. Darleen Opfer and David Pedder (2011), "Most research has concluded that activities that effectively support teachers' professional learning need to be sustained and intensive rather than brief and sporadic" (p. 384). As a structure that is designed to engage teachers in collaborative professional work over an extended period of time, PLCs are more likely to be effective sources of professional growth for teachers than more traditional one-time presentations (Guskey, 2000; Hawley & Valli, 1999; Opfer & Pedder, 2011).

In general, collaboration appears to engender significant professional growth if teachers are willing to explore and analyze important aspects of their practice (Servage, 2008, 2009). The MetLife Survey of the American Teacher found that the majority of teachers believe that collaboration would have a positive effect on their own success and that of their students (MetLife, 2009, 2010). The 2009 survey focused specifically on collaboration and found that:

- Sixty-seven percent of teachers and 78 percent of principals surveyed believe that increased collaboration would significantly impact student achievement

- Ninety percent of teachers surveyed agreed that "other teachers contribute to their success in the classroom" (MetLife, 2009, p. 12)

As a by-product of enhancing teachers' instructional prowess, PLCs can also help establish a culture in which teachers feel more empowered in their work. In a 2009 study by Patricia Hoffman, Anne Dahlman, and Ginger Zierdt, the researchers surveyed fifty-six teachers who had participated in a PLC program and found extremely high rates of agreement with items regarding the experience's positive impacts on their teaching practice as well as their feelings of efficacy. Their findings are summarized in table 1.4.

Table 1.4: PLC Survey Items With High Rates of Agreement

Survey Question	Percentage of Teachers Who Responded "Agree/Strongly Agree"
Participating in a PLC assisted me to develop new knowledge and skills.	95.5
Participating in a PLC helped me establish or strengthen professional networks.	95.5
I felt a sense of belonging in my PLC.	90.0
I believe the PLC was a place where my voice was heard, respected, and valued.	100.0
I believe my participation in the PLC will have a long-term impact.	94.4
My participation in the PLC translated into tangible, concrete actions.	90.0
I believe a PLC is a place to develop a plan of action.	95.5

Source: Adapted from Hoffman et al., 2009, p. 36.

A nationally representative survey of educators by the National Center for Literacy Education (NCLE) found similar correlations between collaboration and "valued professional learning outcomes" (NCLE, 2013, p. 20). Respondents who indicated agreement with the survey item "Collaboration is a routine part of how we do our jobs here" were likely to also agree with statements regarding high levels of trust, exchange of information about best practices, allowance to try new ideas, and use of student data (NCLE, 2013, p. 20).

Although one of the goals of a PLC is to improve teachers' instructional practice, it is important to note that individual improvement alone is not enough. Research suggests that professional learning communities provide a unique, schoolwide perspective on pedagogy (Louis & Marks, 1996; Newmann & Wehlage, 1995). Citing studies by the Center on Organization and Restructuring of Schools, Fred M. Newmann and Gary G. Wehlage (1995) explained that schoolwide "authentic pedagogy . . . calls for channeling individual human commitment and competence into collective organizational productivity. Schools need to have a clear, shared purpose . . . collaborative activity . . . and collective responsibility" (p. 51). Similarly, DuFour and Marzano (2011) suggested that "the focus must shift from helping individuals become more effective in their isolated classrooms and schools, to creating a new collaborative culture based on interdependence, shared responsibility, and mutual accountability" (p. 67). Distributed knowledge, collective capacity, and shared responsibility are much more powerful than the abilities of even the best teachers working in isolation. Research reviewed by the NCLE (2013) found that "a school's social capital—the connections between educators and the extent to which they exchange and build on each other's knowledge—is just as powerful a predictor of student achievement as raw human capital—the skills of individual teachers" (p. 14). Additionally, collaborative structures make the professional learning process more efficient and more sustainable. Teachers can learn from each other's ideas and experiments; when an expert teacher leaves a school, much of his or her knowledge will remain (NCLE, 2013). As mentioned previously, organizational connectedness allows for the storage of tacit knowledge.

A second benefit for teachers in the PLC process is the potential for increased satisfaction with their careers. To better understand this benefit, consider the following model of job satisfaction. Studies summarized by Frederick Herzberg (1987) suggested that satisfaction and dissatisfaction are two separate spectrums, each affected by a distinct set of factors. In this model, not being *dissatisfied* with one's job does not necessarily mean that one is *satisfied*. In the same way, low satisfaction does not mean high dissatisfaction. Job dissatisfaction is affected by "hygiene" factors—basic elements such as company policy, relationships at work, salary, and job security. When these elements are positive, dissatisfaction is low; when these elements are lacking or negative, dissatisfaction increases. Job satisfaction, on the other hand, is affected by "motivators" such as growth, responsibility, recognition, and achievement. As these elements increase, satisfaction increases. Considering these two independent elements (dissatisfaction and satisfaction), it is clear that raising an employee's salary or improving other hygiene factors is not enough to create true job satisfaction—only to decrease dissatisfaction. The factors that contribute to satisfaction require creating opportunities for growth, increased responsibility, and recognition. Table 1.5 displays components that influence satisfaction and dissatisfaction respectively.

Table 1.5: Influences on Job Satisfaction and Dissatisfaction

Satisfaction	Dissatisfaction
Growth	Company policies
Responsibility	Relationships with coworkers
Recognition	Salary
Achievement	Job security

Along these lines, Edward L. Deci and his colleagues (2001) presented a model of job satisfaction and fulfillment that centers on three factors: (1) competence, (2) autonomy, and (3) relatedness. *Competence* means engaging in appropriately challenging tasks (not too difficult or too easy) and achieving success. *Autonomy* means having options and making decisions for oneself. *Relatedness* means interacting with other people and experiencing mutual respect and care. When these factors are met, employees are more likely to be engaged and motivated in their work and experience better overall mental health. PLCs have the potential to increase these motivational factors for teachers. For example, as a result of the collaborative structure inherent in PLCs, teachers have opportunities to make decisions on a regular basis. This empowers teachers and provides autonomy; they do not just receive and carry out directives from administrators. Stated differently, "Decentralization of decision making encourages people to learn because they know they will have the opportunity and, indeed, the responsibility to use their knowledge in their daily activities" (Pfeffer & Sutton, 2000, p. 103). Overall, teachers in schools with higher levels of collaboration are more likely to be very satisfied with teaching as a career (68 percent versus 54 percent in schools with lower levels of collaboration; MetLife, 2009).

As might be inferred from the preceding discussion, PLCs require reconceptualizing one's definition of the job of a teacher. In the United States, it is typical for a teacher to spend nearly all of his or her time instructing students, with a few hours each week spent planning alone (Hord, 1997; NCLE, 2013). In other countries, however, it is more common for teachers to teach fewer classes and spend a significant portion of the work day collaborating with other teachers to plan lessons and improve instruction and learning (Darling-Hammond, 1994, 1997; DuFour & Marzano, 2011; Hord, 1997; NCLE, 2013; Organisation for Economic Co-operation and Development [OECD], 2010).

Regardless of how one imagines the job of a teacher, the fact remains that it is a difficult one. Indeed, Lee Shulman (2004) described teaching as "perhaps the most complex, most challenging, and most demanding, subtle, nuanced, and frightening activity that our species has ever invented" (p. 504) and, in comparing the challenges of teaching to those of other professions, posited that "the only time medicine even approaches the complexity of an average day of classroom teaching is in an emergency room during a natural disaster" (p. 504). In the face of questions about instructional practice, difficult students, and so on, the best resource for a teacher may be his or her colleagues (Rosenholtz, 1991). If one also considers that "teachers' regard for their work—their sense of optimism, hope, and commitment—tends to reside in workplace conditions that enable them to feel professionally empowered and self-fulfilled" (Rosenholtz, 1991, p. 165), it becomes clear that meaningful collaboration can help teachers develop a sense of efficacy and, as a result, help increase student achievement.

Benefits for Students

A growing research base supports the claim that PLCs lead to improved student outcomes. Valerie E. Lee, Julia B. Smith, and Robert G. Croninger (1995, 1997) studied high school students' achievement gains on math and science questions from the National Assessment of Educational Progress and reported that the PLC process "is strongly and positively associated with both effectiveness and equity in learning in both mathematics and science" (1997, p. 139). In both math and science between both eighth and tenth grade and tenth and twelfth grade, students from high schools where teachers had higher levels of collective responsibility achieved greater gains than students from less collaborative schools (1995). These results suggest that when collaborative structures are in place, "more learning occurs" (1997, p. 142). Newmann and Wehlage (1995) found similar results in their study of students' math and social studies performance: the higher the level of professional collaboration at a school, the higher students' achievement.

Karen Seashore Louis and Helen Marks (1996) analyzed data from eight elementary, eight middle, and eight high schools to examine the relationship between the quality of professional community and student achievement. They found moderate correlations between the quality of professional collaboration and both the quality of classroom pedagogy (.36, $P \leq .01$) and student achievement (.26, $P \leq .001$, adjusted for grade level and student background). In other words, "The achievement level is significantly higher to the extent that schools are strong professional communities" (p. 19). The researchers concluded, "Our findings strongly support . . . that the organization of teachers' work in ways that promote professional community will have significant effects on the organization of classrooms for learning and the academic performance of students" (p. 26).

Another study of collaborative schools and students' test results (in this case, scores on the Texas Assessment of Knowledge and Skills) found that the majority of PLC schools reported increases in students' scores over a three-year period. For mathematics, 90.6 percent of PLC schools had increases; for reading and English language arts, 98.4 percent of PLC schools saw their students' scores go up (Hughes & Kritsonis, 2007).

In 2008, Vicki Vescio, Dorene Ross, and Alyson Adams provided the following summary of the effects of learning communities on teachers and students:

> Participation in learning communities impacts teaching practice as teachers become more student centered. In addition, teaching culture is improved because the learning communities increase collaboration, a focus on student learning, teacher authority or empowerment, and continuous learning; [finally,] when teachers participate in a learning community, students benefit as well, as indicated by improved achievement scores over time. (p. 88)

Further research has continued to support these findings. For example, Fulton and Britton (2011) analyzed six previous studies on collaborative structures and student learning in mathematics; all six studies found positive effects. In addition to increased achievement across content areas, studies have shown that PLCs lead to decreased student absences and a lower dropout rate (NCLE, 2013; Newmann & Wehlage, 1995). Positive results in studies of PLCs are also not limited to the United States. In a 2005 study from the University of Bristol in England, researchers found that "pupil learning was the foremost concern of people working in PLCs and the more developed a PLC appeared to be, the more positive was the association with two key measures of effectiveness—pupil achievement and professional learning" (Bolam et al., 2005, p. 146). In short, a wide range of research over several decades has shown that the existence of effective PLCs is associated with enhanced student achievement.

Benefits for Leaders

In addition to providing benefits for teachers and students, PLCs benefit school leaders by increasing their ability to support teacher development and student achievement. The classroom teacher has a direct effect on the achievement of his or her students, but it is also true that leadership at the district and school levels has an effect on student achievement, albeit indirectly (Day et al., 2009; Lee, Louis, & Anderson, 2012; Marzano, Waters, & McNulty, 2005; Witziers, Bosker, & Kruger, 2003).

To illustrate the potentially synergistic effect of PLCs, figure 1.1 displays the relationships among districts, schools, PLCs, instruction, and achievement (Lee et al., 2012). In the figure, solid lines indicate the direct effect of elements over which educators have control; dotted lines represent the influence of contextual factors like grade level and percentage of students eligible for free or reduced lunch. For example, district policies and practices are directly linked to teachers' instructional practices, while school contexts exert an indirect influence. As shown in figure 1.1, districts can only influence student achievement through their influence on teachers. It makes sense, then, that supportive leaders who positively influence teachers can positively influence students (Lee et al., 2012).

Additionally, DuFour and Marzano (2011) provided a perspective on the manner in which PLCs can change interactions between school leaders and teachers. To illustrate, consider figure 1.2, which depicts the manner in which a principal in a school without PLCs affects student achievement. In schools without PLCs, principals and administrators must work with teachers individually to enhance their actions in the classroom, which, in turn, will have a positive effect on student achievement. In a large school with many teachers, this

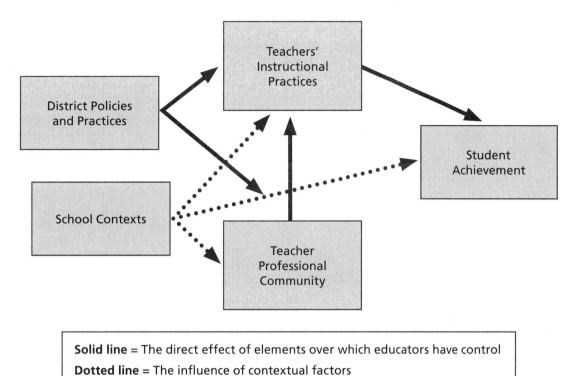

Source: Lee et al., 2012, p. 140. Used with permission.

Figure 1.1: Districts' indirect influence on student achievement.

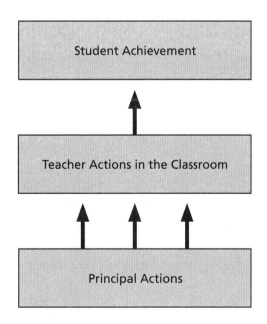

Source: DuFour & Marzano, 2011, p. 49. Used with permission.

Figure 1.2: Typical relationship between principal behavior and student achievement.

quickly becomes unmanageable for the principal. By contrast, in a school that has implemented the PLC process, the principal can more directly influence collaborative teams. The collaborative teams, in turn, have direct influence on teachers' classroom practice, which then affects student achievement (shown in figure 1.3).

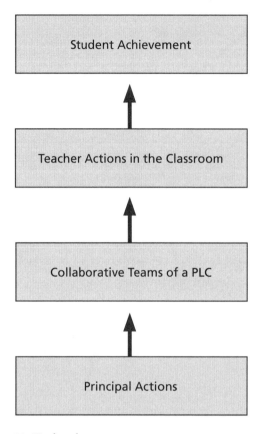

Source: DuFour & Marzano, 2011, p. 52. Used with permission.

Figure 1.3: Relationship between principal behavior and student achievement within PLCs.

In short, professional learning communities allow school and district leaders to have a powerful effect on student achievement.

Translating Research and Theory Into Practice

In the ensuing chapters, we draw on the research and theory presented here to provide practical steps that schools wishing to engage in the PLC process can undertake. As explained previously, we present a new approach to answering DuFour and his colleagues' four critical questions and add two new questions. The complete set is as follows.

1. What is it we want our students to know?

2. How will we know if our students are learning?

3. How will we respond when students do not learn?

4. How will we enrich and extend the learning for students who are proficient?

5.   How will we increase our instructional competence?

6.   How will we coordinate our efforts as a school?

The emphases implicit in these questions are curriculum, assessment, instruction, teacher development, and school leadership.

Each remaining chapter in this book discusses a topic that is essential work for a PLC or collaborative team. Chapter 2 establishes a base for the PLC process through schoolwide structures and processes for productive collaboration. Chapters 3 through 6 examine how collaborative teams can address the identified emphases and transform curriculum, assessment, instruction, and teacher development, respectively. Finally, chapter 7 focuses on the importance of effective leadership in a PLC. Taken together, these elements represent a complete set of guidelines for the PLC process that goes above and beyond previous discussions of the topic.

CHAPTER 2 | Establishing and Maintaining Collaborative Teams

In the first chapter, we were rather loose in our use of terms like *PLC*, *the PLC process*, and *collaborative teams*. We felt that this was necessary because those researchers and practitioners who have written about the PLC concept have used these and related terms in various, idiosyncratic ways. To rectify this issue, we will define and use specific terms in specific ways from here on out. We'll use the term *PLC process* to represent all the policies and practices that lead a school to establish and maintain a network of collaborative teams whose work enhances the learning of students. We'll refer to a PLC as a school that consistently achieves this goal. To this extent, becoming a PLC is a standard to which a school holds itself, celebrating when the standard is met and making adjustments when it is not. Finally, the core of a PLC is the network of *collaborative teams*— the groups of teachers working together to improve student learning. As the title of this book indicates, we believe that collaborative teams have the potential to transform the major aspects of teaching and learning. We begin with a discussion of the context that must surround the establishment and maintenance of collaborative teams.

Schoolwide Norms

In our view, the entire school should operate as a PLC made up of a network of collaborative teams. Those collaborative teams, if they are to function effectively, must be linked by schoolwide norms. *Norms* are the broad descriptors of the behaviors in which all members of the schoolwide effort will engage. They create consistency across the PLC that allows individual teams to operate effectively and efficiently within it. Schoolwide norms are a common suggestion in PLC literature (for example, DuFour & Eaker, 1998; Eaker, DuFour, & DuFour, 2002; Hord & Sommers, 2008). The following sample set is representative of most lists.

- School leaders create supportive conditions so teachers and students can focus on the core concern of learning.

- Teachers work collaboratively on the key aspects of curriculum, assessment, and instruction; monitor what students are achieving; and use that information to enhance instruction.

- Students understand that their school will not let them fail—their teachers will provide time and support when they are at risk of failing or disengaging.

- Teachers inform parents about the progress of their children on a regular basis.

- Stakeholders support the idea that each student can and will be successful.

- School leaders and teachers monitor progress on an ongoing basis.

The essential idea behind these norms is that the organization as a whole is committed to working together to improve student learning. The range of stakeholders involved (teachers, students, parents, and administrators) points to the fact that the PLC process typically works best when the entire school community participates. Stated differently, a group of teachers meeting regularly does not constitute a PLC; rather, the entire school should function in a collaborative and purposeful manner. Here we consider a few selected norms that are critical to the PLC process.

One important schoolwide norm is that "teachers and staff have formal ways to provide input regarding the optimal functioning of the school" (Marzano, Warrick, & Simms, 2014, p. 15). When school leaders seek input from teachers and staff, the school can become more effective (Marzano et al., 2005). This norm has the dual benefit of increasing teacher buy-in and improving leaders' decision making. When teachers are involved in the changes and decisions, they feel more ownership of and commitment to the process. School leaders improve their decision-making abilities by gathering more information, opinions, and options than they could alone. Just as teacher collaborative teams improve their effectiveness by working together, school leaders can do the same by collaborating with teachers and staff. Formal protocols for input might include paper or online feedback forms, committees, and regular opportunities for face-to-face conversations.

Another important schoolwide norm is that "collaborative groups regularly interact to address common issues regarding curriculum, assessment, instruction, and the achievement of all students" (Marzano et al., 2014, p. 15). This idea is the core of the PLC concept. Staff are expected to collaborate, learn, help, share, and be an integral part of the school community. We suggest that if a school is to function effectively as a PLC, a teacher's or staff member's participation in the PLC process be considered an essential job function. Collaboration is nonnegotiable in a productive PLC; staff cannot and do not opt out (DuFour & Marzano, 2011; Marzano & Waters, 2009).

Some PLC proponents use the term itself to establish schoolwide norms by considering the meanings of the words *professional*, *learning*, and *community*. For example, a school unpacking the meaning of the term *PLC* might conclude that *professional* learning communities require staff to treat their work as a profession by utilizing research and outside knowledge and embracing improvement. Professional *learning* communities ask teachers to view themselves as learners and co-contributors to each other's learning. Professional learning *communities* operate with collaboration as their foundational commitment by regularly working together on school and classroom issues, expressly seeking to learn through collaboration, and using dialogue to advance their capabilities for the benefit of students. The staff and administration of the school might further conclude that *community* implies a group of people unified by a common interest; in the case of a PLC, the commonalities include commitment to ensuring student learning by enhancing professional practice.

On the whole, the schoolwide norms that guide the PLC process are quite different from those that usually govern more traditional schools. Schools that endeavor to become PLCs must transition from teachers who work in isolation to teachers who work in collaboration and from stakeholders who think in terms of "my responsibility" to those who think in terms of "our responsibility" (DuFour & Marzano, 2011).

Schoolwide Structures

By its very nature, the PLC process involves the creation of specific structures. The two structures we detail here are time-based considerations and the formation of collaborative teams.

Collaborative Time

Certainly, the major topic for restructuring is how to provide time to collaborate. This can be challenging, but if a school values collaboration, allotted time is essential for putting that value into practice. In the United States, public perception tends to assume that teachers who are not instructing a class are not working. As mentioned previously, American teachers typically spend far more time instructing students than teachers in many other countries (Darling-Hammond, 1994, 1997; DuFour & Marzano, 2011; Hord, 1997; NCLE, 2013; OECD, 2010); teachers around the world are often given substantial time during the work day to plan and collaborate with colleagues (OECD, 2010). In fact, in the countries that achieved the greatest degree of educational progress between 1980 and 2010, teachers were given between fifteen and twenty-five hours per week to engage in the type of work typical of the PLC process (Darling-Hammond, 2010; DuFour & Marzano, 2011). To change a culture of isolation into a culture of collaboration, teachers first need the time to collaborate.

A variety of structures can be implemented to allow for collaborative time. For example, teachers within a collaborative group might have common planning time during the school day. Some schools employ late-start or early-out schedules for students and use that time for teacher collaboration. Some schools find it most helpful to identify several structures that allow for collaborative time and use multiple strategies to provide staff with regular opportunities to collaborate. The following vignette depicts how one school provided time for collaborative teams to interact.

> Carlson Charter School employs a delayed-start schedule one day every two weeks to provide time for collaborative teams to meet. Using a late-start option works well in this situation because the regular school day, a four-period block schedule, starts at 9:05 a.m. By using a delayed start of just twenty minutes, teachers gain collaborative time from 8:15 to 9:20 a.m., which is still within the parameters of the contracted work day.
>
> Although classes start twenty minutes later, students are still bussed to campus at the regular time, so many students still arrive on campus at the time they normally would. To supervise the campus during the delayed starts, administrators, resource officers, teacher assistants, and parent volunteers oversee activities. The late start also provides a time for counselors to meet with students without pulling them out of class.
>
> The dates for delayed starts are marked on the school calendar to remind parents that regular classes begin at 9:25 a.m. on those days. Consequently, the delayed-start days also provide an opportunity for students to schedule medical and other appointments and still arrive at school on time so attendance is not affected.

continued →

Regular Schedule		Delayed Start Schedule	
		Collaborative time	8:15 to 9:20
Period 1	9:05 to 10:30	Period 1	9:25 to 10:45
Period 2	10:38 to 12:03	Period 2	10:53 to 12:13
Lunch	12:11 to 12:31	Lunch	12:21 to 12:41
Period 3	12:39 to 2:04	Period 3	12:49 to 2:09
Period 4	2:12 to 3:37	Period 4	2:17 to 3:37

Regardless of how and when collaborative time is provided, a school's teachers and administrators must view that time as essential and inviolable. That is, collaborative time should never be sacrificed for other purposes—the collaborative team meeting is the core of the PLC process.

In addition to making time for collaborative team meetings, schools also need to implement other structures in their schedules to support the PLC process. For example, regular intervention time, during which collaborative teams provide remediation to struggling students or enrichment for students who have achieved proficiency, is another key structure within the PLC process. Collaborative teams identify students for intervention based on common assessment results. During intervention time, one or more teachers from the team provide extra instruction to these students, while the others provide extension activities for students who have achieved proficiency. Intervention time is often scheduled by administrators on a schoolwide basis; however, it could also be implemented by individual collaborative teams. In either case, as with collaborative meeting time, intervention time should be one of the first things reserved in the schedule.

As a part of the scheduling process, school leaders should also have regular meetings with collaborative teams in some capacity. This interaction might involve the administrator attending a portion of the team's meeting or meeting separately with a collaborative team leader or representative. The purpose of these meetings is to maintain a strong connection between teachers and leaders. In this way, school leaders have a regular opportunity to efficiently influence teaching practices while staying up to date with the successes and needs of teams and individual teachers.

Finally, protocols should be in place to ensure that the school operates as a true network of collaborative teams. In other words, communication and collaboration should occur not only within teams or between leaders and individual teams but also between various teams. These protocols might include discussing PLC topics at all-staff meetings or establishing a recurring meeting with school leaders to which each collaborative team sends a representative. These structures for time and communication are critical foundations that support the creation and work of collaborative teams themselves.

Collaborative Teams

A central assumption of this book is that organizing teachers and staff into meaningful collaborative teams is a foundational step in the PLC process. Given its importance, we address the issue here and again in chapter 7 (page 103). There, we approach the issue from the perspective of common mistakes that schools becoming PLCs make. Here, we consider frequently used approaches. No two schools are exactly alike in terms of what constitutes a meaningful team. The most commonly used structures are grade-level teams and content-area teams, but schools can use other organizational schemes to suit their needs. All structures have strengths and weaknesses. For example, content-area teams are more likely to achieve a deeper focus on the technical aspects of their subjects, but cross-disciplinary teams can still do meaningful subject-specific work while also dealing with broader pedagogical issues and opportunities for learning across content areas (Fulton & Britton, 2011).

Groups should be regularly and easily formed. Many schools begin with a horizontal grouping—teachers from a single grade level, regardless of content area—or a vertical grouping—teachers from a single content area but several grade levels. Of course, these groupings depend a great deal on the size of a building. If a school only has one first-grade teacher, then grouping by grade bands (grades K–2, for example) makes logical sense. Some schools choose to use a team structure in which teachers from different content areas teach a common group of students. Such a team might consist of a math teacher, an ELA teacher, a science teacher, a social studies teacher, and a special education teacher who all serve a common group of eighth graders. Such a team could clearly focus on common issues around curriculum, assessment, and instruction. Marvin Fairman and Leon McLean (2003) recommended creating teams by considering the stakeholders who are closest to the point of implementation and who will be responsible for applying and implementing decisions made by the team.

In terms of team structure, a substantial portion of the research and theory focuses on teachers—particularly teachers of academic subjects—as the sole members of collaborative teams (Bolam et al., 2005). In many schools, however, support staff, special education teachers, and teachers of so-called nonacademic subjects are rightfully recognized as essential to the success of all students and are therefore included in collaborative team structures. When expanding membership in collaborative teams, it is important to note that inclusion in the PLC process or collaborative teams should not be limited to those staff members who are enthusiastic about the idea. Whatever the constitution of collaborative teams, the PLC process requires a degree of commitment from all stakeholders (Hord, 1997; Louis et al., 1995).

An interesting factor to consider when creating teams of teachers and staff is the rapport and relationships between various members. Tom Rath and Donald O. Clifton (2009) asserted that "people with best friends at work have better safety records, receive higher customer satisfaction scores, and increase workplace productivity" (p. 77). Collaborative teams have great potential for increasing positive personal relationships as teachers work together to improve instruction, assessment, and student achievement. As in all things, however, balance is important. Although it is important for team members to have amicable relationships, the interactions within collaborative teams must go beyond collegiality or friendship, as the purpose of these groups is to engage in critical inquiry. Teachers and staff who are close friends or very social with each other may be less likely to remain open to new ideas, ask difficult questions, or push their peers to improve (Achinstein, 2002; Granovetter, 1973; Lee et al., 2012; Mindich & Lieberman, 2012). Dan Mindich and Ann Lieberman (2012) summarized this potential pitfall by saying, "Positive staff relations can help create the base for PLCs, but they can also create a sense that further collaborative work is not needed" (p. 38). Collaborative teams should also include a representation of diverse viewpoints. Teachers may prefer to work with colleagues who are very similar to themselves in terms of content area, teaching style, or other factors. If members of a collaborative team are too similar, however, it can also defeat the critical purpose of the group (Elbousty & Bratt, 2010). Considering these factors when creating teams can be helpful toward maximizing the potential for success. The following vignette depicts strategies one school used to group teachers into collaborative teams.

Merriam High School employs two collaborative team structures to best serve its students. Ninth-grade students are divided into teams to create a sense of community within a large incoming class transitioning from four different middle schools. Each student team is taught by a cross-curricular collaborative team, consisting of teachers in math, English, science, social studies, and special education. These ninth-grade collaborative teams operate with a focus on student achievement and work collaboratively to plan necessary interventions for students within their respective teams. As cross-curricular teams, they vigilantly monitor achievement trends for their common set of students. That is, a team looks at students' results across the core subject areas to identify academically at-risk freshmen before the students fail multiple classes. Then, a team works together on academic interventions to help these students. For example, an entire collaborative team often conducts common parent-teacher conferences for students who are doing poorly in several subjects.

Instructionally, these ninth-grade teams collaborate to find cross-curricular content linkages and make relevant connections for students. For example, if students are studying a specific region of the world in social studies, English teachers might use literature from that region in their language arts lessons. In some cases, these cross-curricular connections provide common assessment opportunities as well. One example of this is the study of a topic in biology corresponding with the writing of a research paper in English. Students work on finding source information in their biology class and then organize and write the paper during their English class. Teachers use the completed research paper as a common assessment for both classes. The science teacher assesses the science content and research design, while the English teacher assesses the writing and organization.

The second collaborative team structure this school uses involves teachers of the upper grades who all teach the same courses, such as tenth-grade English, physics, or algebra II. These teams also focus on student achievement with a greater emphasis on the development of common formative assessments and common interventions based on assessment results. Each of these teams also establishes student achievement goals related to the school's overall improvement goals. For example, an algebra I collaborative team develops the following student achievement goal: achieve an overall passing rate of at least 80 percent on the state test given in May. This goal supports the schoolwide improvement goal of increasing overall student performance in all areas of math by 5 percent as measured by state testing. To monitor progress toward this goal, the team uses common formative assessments to measure students' passing rates throughout the school year. When these results show it to be necessary, they collaborate on intervention and extension lessons.

Culture Within Collaborative Teams

We have already mentioned the importance of schoolwide processes and norms, but for individual collaborative teams to operate effectively, they must also develop a specific culture within their teams. Michael Fullan (2008) emphasized the importance of culture when he asserted that "*positive* purposeful peer interaction" (p. 45) is most likely to occur when three specific conditions are in place:

(1) when the larger values of the organization and those of individuals and groups mesh; (2) when information and knowledge about effective practices are widely and openly shared; and (3) when monitoring mechanisms are in place to detect and address ineffective actions while also identifying and consolidating effective practices. (p. 45)

The first two of Fullan's three conditions—shared values and shared practices—are at the heart of effective collaborative teams. While structures (such as time to meet) and administrative support are important, they alone cannot create effective collaborative teams (AISR, 2004). A culture that promotes meaningful collaboration is essential.

In 2009, Hoffman and her colleagues published the results of a three-year study of five PLCs formed as part of a partnership between a university and several local school districts. Their findings shed light on the processes collaborative teams might use to establish an effective culture. The collaborative teams in this study all followed the same basic process: members established group functions and ground rules, developed trust, then focused on reading research and conducting projects relevant to their group. The researchers identified the following factors as important to culture: prior planning, diversity of participants, shared leadership, respect, group norms, and responsiveness to questions and issues. Establishing these factors was an important first step for the teams, one that had to take place before they could engage in meaningful work.

Establishing the culture of a collaborative team is also an ongoing process. Collaborative teams always have the potential for success and for dysfunction, simply because they are made up of human beings (Lencioni, 2002). A successful collaborative team is not self-sustaining; it requires continuous care and attention: "Indeed, any complacency and slackening of effort might jeopardise the collective operation of the PLC that had been achieved. The promotional and sustaining effort could never cease because both the contexts and the PLCs themselves never ceased evolving" (Bolam et al., 2005, p. 73). Once norms and cultural practices are in place, they must be monitored for adherence and the need for adaptation.

Under the umbrella of culture, we suggest three elements that should be continually monitored.

1. Group norms

2. Trust and relationships

3. Productive collaboration

The following sections address each of these facets in more detail.

Group Norms

Similar to schoolwide norms, group norms are the guiding principles by which a collaborative team governs itself and its work. Norms help validate the purposes of the team and provide a reminder of how team members have agreed to work with one another. Norms serve not only to inspire groups but also to keep them focused (Mindich & Lieberman, 2012). Examples of norms established by collaborative teams include the following.

• Expect all teachers to contribute to the team.

• Handle problems when they are still small.

• Recognize effort, not just results.

• Listen fully with the intention to understand.

- Share "air space"—give everyone the chance to contribute.

- Support the decisions of the group, even if the outcome was not your first choice.

- Respect the privacy of team members by asking before you share something beyond the team.

- Have courageous conversations! Don't be afraid to speak your mind.

One of the first tasks that a newly established collaborative team should undertake is to generate a set of their own norms. It is important that each collaborative team generate their own norms. To do so, the team might hold a brainstorming session. Team members suggest various group norms, perhaps drawing inspiration from other teams of which they have been a part. The team might consider specific questions, such as the following.

- What behaviors do we expect to see frequently?

- What behaviors are unacceptable?

- How do we want to handle problems when they arise?

Teams should also consider norms that address emotional, social, and physical safety. Emotional safety norms might include "Know everyone's names," "Be willing to take others' perspectives," and "Listen actively." Social safety norms might govern issues like confidentiality, open discussions and decision making, or gossip. While true physical safety is likely covered in a school's employee handbook, a group might decide to enhance their physical environment by creating norms around the cleanliness, organization, and sufficiency of their meeting space.

Another powerful strategy that teams can use to come up with norms is to identify behaviors that are undesirable or counterproductive to collaboration. Once the team has described these behaviors, the team can flip them to create positively stated norms. For example, a team may recognize that being late to meetings is an issue. The norm to discourage this would simply become "We will be punctual." As another example, a team might decide that using one's cell phone, laptop, or tablet for personal reasons during a meeting is disrespectful. When flipped, the norm becomes "We will only use technology to support the goals of the meeting."

As the team brainstorms, one member should record all suggestions, ideally on chart paper or a whiteboard so the whole group can see and review the suggestions. If there are many suggestions, the group might work together to combine related options and create a more manageable list of norms. The team then collaborates to agree on the most important norms, which will become the adopted set of norms. There are many ways to go about this, such as engaging in a simple discussion, having members vote on their top three norms, or distributing stickers and having members indicate their votes on the chart paper. At the end of this process, the group should have between four and ten agreed-upon norms. Once they establish the final list of norms, the group should create a description of each one, perhaps using "looks like" and "sounds like" to describe how the norm will manifest. As a last step, the team should take the time to discuss how they will hold one another accountable for the norms. For example, how will they celebrate when their team abides by the norms for a designated period of time? Contrastingly, how will they solve the problem if norms are disregarded?

After norms have been established, it is important to monitor adherence to them over time. This might be accomplished by having members periodically rate the group's adherence to norms (for example, on a 1–4 scale). Figure 2.1 shows an example of what a norm-monitoring form might look like.

Norm	Example	Nonexample	Rating
Demonstrate respect for one another and our mutual learning.	Team members are supportive of others trying new instructional strategies.	Team members are disrespectful of the group by resisting new ideas.	
Listen fully with the intention to understand.	Team members practice active listening skills, such as attending to the speaker, rephrasing for clarity, and asking questions.	Team members engage in side conversations while others are speaking.	
Participate and contribute actively.	All team members take part in discussions, offering ideas and reacting to others' thoughts.	One or more team members often disengage from the conversation.	
Enter discussions with an open mind.	Team members fairly consider the merit of all proposed ideas.	Team members refuse to consider certain ideas.	
Share air space.	All team members participate somewhat equally in discussion.	One or two people dominate the conversation.	
Maintain confidentiality.	Team members only discuss student and/or teacher data within team meetings.	A teacher distributes student data or information about another team member outside the group.	
Follow time allocations.	The team focuses on each topic for the amount of time specified on the agenda.	Discussions of specific topics often run too long; as a result, other topics are ignored.	
Make decisions by consensus.	The team takes a vote on specific issues.	One team member imposes his or her decisions on the rest.	
Support decisions.	All team members accept the group's consensus, even if it was not their first choice.	Team members who disagree with the group's consensus refuse to take part.	
Have courageous conversations.	The team proactively discusses difficult topics before they become larger problems.	The team does not talk about things that are bothering them.	

Figure 2.1: Example norm-monitoring chart.

The rating scale shown in figure 2.1 allows individuals to evaluate how well the group has been abiding by specific norms. It allows the team to look at trends in the scores to identify areas for celebration and improvement. Lower scores like 1 or 2 would suggest that the team should either review a norm's importance or revisit the need for it. Reflection upon the pre-existing norms and how they are working is essential for efficient and effective team operations. Such scrutiny can be a reminder to modify, add, or delete norms so that they are more representative of the needs of the group. The power of norms is not in creating them, but in following them. Appendix B (page 125) contains resources teams can use to create and monitor norms.

Trust and Relationships

For collaborative teams (and, indeed, entire schools or organizations) to function optimally, group members must trust each other. One might describe trust by saying, "I can show you my true self and know that you won't take advantage of me" (Eurich, 2013, p. 24). It is sometimes easier to identify the absence of trust than it is to identify the presence of trust.

When collaborative teams do not have trust, group members tend to blame each other when problems occur instead of working together to fix them. Nontrusting team members waste energy worrying or trying to position themselves to look good relative to their peers. They are often anxious about speaking up, feeling unable to share their honest opinions. On the other hand, when trust *is* present, it can positively affect group performance. A study by Kurt T. Dirks (1999) found that "trust appeared to influence how motivation was translated into group process and performance. That is, in high-trust groups, motivation was transformed into joint efforts and hence higher performance, in low-trust groups, motivation was transformed into individual efforts" (Dirks, 1999, p. 453). Stated differently, when people trust each other, they can collaborate more effectively. Tasha Eurich (2013) described two types of trust that can be helpful for teams: competence-based trust and motive-based trust. *Competence-based trust* refers to people regarding each other as competent and reliable. They are knowledgeable about relevant topics and follow through on stated tasks. *Motive-based trust* refers to a person's belief that someone has positive intentions. Clearly, both these elements are essential for trusting relationships.

In their book *Trust in Schools*, Anthony S. Bryk and Barbara Schneider (2002) posited a model of relational trust (that is, trust between people based on both beliefs and observations) in which people discern the trustworthiness of others based on four factors.

1. **Respect:** Does this person acknowledge that I also have an important role to play here?
2. **Competence:** Can this person do his or her job effectively?
3. **Personal regard for others:** Does this person care about the people around him or her?
4. **Integrity:** Does this person follow through on what he or she says?

The degree to which each of these factors is present in a collaborative team makes up the overall atmosphere of trust. If one element is significantly lacking, no amount of the others can entirely make up for it.

One simple tactic for building trust and good relationships between team members is for each person to share some details about him- or herself. When colleagues know each other as people, rather than just as coworkers, they are more inclined to trust each other. Another method is to conduct short team-building activities on a regular basis. Quick, engaging activities can instill the team with shared purpose, appreciation for differences, and an element of enjoyment. Additionally, each team member should strive to demonstrate trustworthiness and qualities such as those identified by Eurich (2013) and by Bryk and Schneider (2002). For example, teachers might focus on the following recommendations.

- Take responsibility for your own words and actions. Do not make excuses; apologize when necessary.

- Arrive on time to meetings, and respond to email and other correspondence in a timely manner.

- Share relevant information candidly and transparently with the entire team.

Developing trust is a process, but it is essential for effective teamwork. Teams that use the strategies described in this section can put aside individual differences and focus on team accomplishments that serve students.

Productive Collaboration

Productive collaboration refers to the quality and depth of interactions between team members:

> All teacher interactions are not the same; professional discussions vary greatly in their degree of depth. Prior research suggests that typical conversations in teachers' professional communities are of low depth, characterized by story swapping, sharing materials, and providing discrete bits of information or advice. . . . In contrast, high depth interactions focused on the pedagogical principles underlying instructional approaches [and] the nature of students' . . . thinking. (Coburn & Russell, 2008, pp. 1–2)

Clearly, the majority of collaborative team work should fall into the category of high-depth interactions: discussing research-based instructional strategies, planning lessons, reviewing assessment data, and so on. To ensure this, protocols for productive collaboration should be set up from the beginning and their implementation monitored over time. Appendix B (page 125) includes resources to help teams focus on the right work.

In the course of PLC work, teams will necessarily discuss sensitive issues. Productive collaboration does not mean that everyone agrees all the time. In fact, it often means the opposite—frequent respectful disagreement is necessary. Groups that avoid healthy conflict cannot fully discuss an issue, and faked agreement can lead to superficiality. Robert J. Garmston and Bruce M. Wellman (2009) promoted the concept of *cognitive conflict*. They explained that "meetings must be safe but not necessarily comfortable. . . . Cognitive conflict—disagreements among group members about substantive issues . . . —tend[s] to improve team effectiveness, lead to better decisions, and increase commitment, cohesiveness, empathy, and understanding" (p. 68). Cognitive conflict is different from personal conflict. Group members should argue about ideas, rather than with each other.

The ability to disagree respectfully is obviously related to trust: if group members do not trust each other, they may not speak honestly in order to avoid vulnerability or potential ridicule (Lencioni, 2002). To ensure discussions remain respectfully productive, it is useful to establish guidelines for interaction. Teams should avoid "unproductive patterns of listening, responding, and inquiring" (Garmston & Wellman, 2009, p. 28), which include autobiographical patterns (telling personal stories around a topic), inquisitive patterns (focusing too closely on noncritical issues), and solution patterns (jumping to a solution too quickly) (Garmston & Wellman, 2009). These negative discussion practices derail the conversation and inhibit good decision making. Other common but destructive discussion practices include assuming that silence means agreement, allowing a few people to dominate, and engaging in side conversations (Mackin, 2007).

It can be difficult for people to raise concerns or conflicting viewpoints about an idea without seeming combative or shutting down the person who posed the original idea. Discussion participants can use the following strategies (Davey, 2013) to disagree politely and without abruptly terminating the conversation.

- **Use *and* rather than *but* when expressing contradiction.** Employ this technique to acknowledge that, when two people express opinions, it is not necessarily true that one is right and one is wrong. For example, "I hear you saying that we should try this hands-on experiment with our students, and I wonder if we have enough materials for every class."

- **Express opposing viewpoints in hypothetical terms.** Ask teammates to imagine the effects or consequences of a particular situation. For example, "What if we could get an expert from the community to come in? What would be the best way to structure the lesson in that situation?"

- **Raise the question of impact.** Ask open-ended questions about how a course of action might turn out. For example, "We're discussing the option of having students work in groups on this; how will that impact their learning?"

- **Elicit underlying reasons.** Seek to better understand an opinion by asking questions that drive at the reasons, goals, or rationale behind it. For example, "Your suggestion to have students take assessments on the computer is interesting; can you explain your reasons for suggesting that?"

Appendix B (page 125) contains additional resources that can help teams engage in polite yet honest and in-depth discussions.

As with other aspects of culture, productive collaboration should be monitored regularly. One way to address this is through a survey. Each member of the team completes the survey individually and anonymously. Example survey items might include the following.

- I feel valued as a part of this team.

- My teammates listen to one another, even when ideas are contrary.

- I enjoy being a part of my collaborative team.

- My collaborative team addresses our agenda items in an efficient and effective manner.

Once all members of the group have completed the survey, the data can be reviewed to determine what the collaborative team is doing well and which issues must be addressed.

In addition to directly addressing these three aspects of team culture (group norms, trust and relationships, and productive collaboration), it is important for teams to be aware of the difficulties of the PLC process. In particular, teams should anticipate common frustrations and the possibility of resistant team members.

Common Frustrations

Transitioning to and working in a collaborative team structure can be a frustrating process. It is unwise for educators to expect otherwise; rather, they should be aware of common difficulties so as not to become discouraged when such difficulties arise. Parry Graham and William M. Ferriter (2010) identified three general causes of frustrations during the transition into the PLC process. The first is time. Already in short supply in schools, time constraints can become even tighter in a PLC and in collaborative teams. Decision making in a group naturally takes longer than individual decision making. Graham and Ferriter (2010) explained:

> As organizations become more collaborative, there is a trade-off between efficiency and effectiveness. Hierarchical organizations, in which a few people at the top make decisions that everyone else follows, are highly efficient . . . but, they also allow little room for creativity and organizational learning. Collaborative organizations in which people work together

to make decisions and learn from each other produce more effective decisions but are much less efficient. (p. 129)

However, it is worth noting that PLCs can also save time through common planning and materials.

The second common cause of frustration is social and philosophical friction. When people work closely together to make and implement decisions, their differing personalities, perspectives, and philosophies can create potential conflict. Additionally, decisions made in a collaborative team affect the entire group (that is, members cannot simply ignore the decision), so individuals are more likely to speak up when they disagree.

The third cause of frustration is increased responsibility and accountability. The PLC process shifts a school from top-down decision making to distributed leadership. While this is generally a good thing, it does increase teachers' responsibilities, which can cause stress. The PLC process requires teachers to look closely at results and be more accountable for ensuring that all students learn.

Graham and Ferriter (2010) made several recommendations regarding how to deal with these frustrations, beyond simply being aware of them. The first is, "Be patient." No one should expect instant results; becoming effective collaborators takes time. Their second recommendation is to closely monitor important areas of collaborative work, such as identification of learning goals, development of common assessments, and collection of data on student learning. Their third recommendation is to acknowledge that veteran teachers may feel more frustrated than their newer colleagues. Beginning teachers have fewer established teaching practices and find a great deal of support and professional learning opportunities through collaborative teams. Veteran teachers, on the other hand, may be asked to discard lesson and unit plans they have been using for years and might feel as though collaboration means they are forced to "mentor less capable teachers" (Elbousty & Bratt, 2010, p. 5), thereby carrying more than their fair share of the weight. The fourth recommendation is to support and simplify collaboration using technology. There are many tools available that allow teams to share resources and work together outside of limited meeting time, such as shared online documents. These tools can help alleviate the issue of limited time.

Resistant Team Members

A final important issue regarding collaborative teams is resistant team members—teachers who would prefer to continue working in isolation, as is traditional for teachers. One way to encourage resistant or negative team members to collaborate is by assigning responsibility (Whitaker, 2002). Often, when someone is difficult to work with, one's instinct is to pull away from that person and avoid involving him or her in tasks. This reaction, however, actually reinforces the person's difficult behavior. Instead, give the difficult person a specific task to accomplish, ideally one that (a) is fairly easy to achieve, and (b) obliges other people to depend on the difficult person. For example, a team might ask a difficult member to type up the agenda or provide the snacks for the next meeting. These types of tasks are simple, ensuring a high likelihood of success, and include a social aspect, increasing both the pressure to complete the task and the social reward for success. The goal in giving responsibility to a reluctant team member is to get that person to successfully do something for which the rest of the group can positively recognize and thank him or her. This recognition helps the person feel valued and useful rather than excluded, increasing his or her motivation to become an effective team member (Whitaker, 2002).

A close relative of responsibility is accountability. A classic example of a complaint from a teacher who shirks accountability is, "I could teach my students if only their previous teachers had done a better job" (Whitaker, 2002). A reluctant teacher might blame the administration for forcing him or her to change "the way I've always done things." In this context, other teachers on the team can reinforce the notion that such excuses will not be tolerated. Collaborative teams should consider creating (or re-emphasizing) norms like the following: "We do not pass blame" or "We approach problems by asking what we can do with what we have, rather than complaining about what is getting in our way."

Another approach to addressing reluctant team members is simply to discourage the type of pessimistic commentary that they usually engage in (Whitaker, 2002). While venting—recounting a frustrating story to get it off one's chest and then moving on—can be a healthy practice, the team meeting is not an appropriate venue. Venting should be directed at one's superior (who may have the power to change the frustrating situation) or to a close personal friend (who can listen and console in confidence). Venting to colleagues of equal or lower rank spreads negativity and is not a productive use of time during a collaborative team meeting. Additionally, negative team members often engage in commentary that would not qualify as productive venting; rather, they gossip, complain, or otherwise make comments that negatively affect the group environment and the team's ability to get work done. Group conversational norms should include rules regarding productive commentary. Comments made only to disparage an idea, person, or situation should be disallowed. If a team member wants to make a complaint or express discontent about something, he or she should also offer a suggestion for how to improve it. When these norms are in place, team members can use them to gently remind a negative colleague of the expectations.

Finally, if reluctant teammates are ever to change their ways, they must have good relationships with the rest of the group. This means that teams should seek to communicate positively whenever possible—acknowledging small successes, inviting participation, and so on. Some researchers suggest the ratio of five positive comments for every one negative or corrective comment as the ideal rate for classroom management (Flora, 2000; Kern, White, & Gresham, 2007; Reinke, Herman, & Stormont, 2013), personal relationships (Gottman, 1994), and collegial relationships (Losada & Heaphy, 2004).

Summary

This chapter has addressed the schoolwide context in which collaborative teams should be developed and nurtured. It also addressed the important features of a well-formed collaborative team. Specific topics included establishing teams and providing structural considerations (such as time for meetings). Once teams are formed, they must work continuously to maintain a productive culture. The next chapter—with a focus on curriculum—begins our discussion of the work in which collaborative teams should engage.

Chapter 2 Comprehension Questions

1. Why are schoolwide norms important?

2. Identify three structures that should be allowed for in a PLC schedule. What are common ways that schools make time for these structures?

3. Describe two common structures for collaborative teams. What are the pros and cons of each?

4. Explain the importance of the following three aspects of collaborative team culture and give an example of how a team might establish and monitor each one.

   A. Group norms

   B. Trust and relationships

   C. Productive collaboration

5. Describe one challenging aspect of the PLC process and how it can be mitigated.

Self-Evaluation for Chapter 2

	Strongly Disagree	Disagree	Neither Agree nor Disagree	Agree	Strongly Agree
1. We have established schoolwide norms that focus on a collective effort to improve student learning.					
2. We have established the structures necessary for the PLC process, including:					
• Collaborative teams					
• A schedule that provides collaborative time					
• Distributed leadership					
3. We have established collaborative team norms.					
4. We continually monitor adherence to norms.					
5. We seek to develop trust among team members.					
6. We have set up processes for productive collaboration, including:					
• Healthy discussion guidelines					
• Efficient work procedures					

CHAPTER 3 | Transforming Curriculum

As mentioned in the first chapter (page 3), current approaches to curriculum can be transformed by an effectual response to the question, What do we want our students to know? We propose that a well-crafted answer to this question begins with a guaranteed and viable curriculum.

The Need for a Guaranteed and Viable Curriculum

The concept of a guaranteed and viable curriculum was first introduced in the book *What Works in Schools* (Marzano, 2003) and was further developed in a number of later publications (for example, DuFour & Marzano, 2011; Marzano et al., 2005; Marzano et al., 2014). By *guaranteed*, we mean that the same content is taught in all classrooms. To achieve this, the curriculum must provide "clear guidance regarding the content to be addressed in specific courses and at specific grade levels" (Marzano et al., 2014, p. 69). A prerequisite to a guaranteed curriculum is a *viable* curriculum—one with content that can be taught in the time available to teachers.

Collaborative teams and a guaranteed and viable curriculum have a symbiotic relationship. If one of the crucial objectives of the PLC process is to increase the quality of students' learning, then a guaranteed and viable curriculum is a foundational element to that mission. Given that a great deal of the collaborative team's work centers on monitoring teacher instruction and student achievement, it is imperative that the team's members have a clear understanding of what they will teach. Without a guaranteed and viable curriculum, assessment tasks and the measurements based on them become inconsistent, invalid, and unreliable. A guaranteed and viable curriculum can only be created, implemented, and sustained through collaborative effort, making this task ideal work for collaborative teams (DuFour & Marzano, 2011). Such activity also creates the opportunity for teachers—those who will eventually deliver the content to students—to be directly involved in curriculum design (DuFour & Marzano, 2011).

The creation of a guaranteed and viable curriculum has four steps, as follows.

1. Identify essential content.

2. Include cognitive and conative skills.

3. Identify learning goals and objectives.

4. Construct proficiency scales.

The following sections discuss these steps in more detail.

Identifying Essential Content

The first step in creating a guaranteed and viable curriculum is to identify the essential content, often called *prioritized standards*. Sets of academic content standards (such as state-designed standards, the Common Core, the Next Generation Science Standards, and others) typically articulate far more content than is possible to teach in the time available. At the beginning of the 21st century, Marzano (2003) estimated that there are about 9,042 hours of instructional time in K–12 education, but the standards (current at that time) would take 15,465 hours to teach. This trend of disparity between content requirements and available instructional time has continued (see Marzano, Yanoski, Hoegh, & Simms, 2013). That is, even with the adoption of new state standards or national models, the problem of too much content is still rampant. As such, it is crucial that collaborative teams distill the broad standards presented by their state or district down to a manageable amount of essential content.

A collaborative team might do this by looking at each standard for their grade level and content area, having each teacher choose the standards (or parts of standards) he or she thinks are essential, and then discussing and coming to a consensus as to which content is essential. More specifically, teams can use a four-step process (Heflebower, Hoegh, & Warrick, 2014) that includes: (1) analyzing the standards to become familiar with the material; (2) individually rating the priority of each standard; (3) grouping the high-priority standards into topics; and (4) reviewing the grouped standards and adjusting as necessary. (For a more detailed discussion, see Heflebower et al., 2014.) The power of this four-step process for rating standards is that all teachers involved have the opportunity to weigh in on the decisions. Additionally, as they make decisions about priority standards, content knowledge across all group members increases.

As a measure for determining the importance of individual standards, groups can use Larry Ainsworth's (2003) criteria: endurance, leverage, and readiness. *Endurance* refers to whether or not the knowledge and skills will be valuable over time. *Leverage* refers to the usefulness of the knowledge and skills in multiple disciplines. *Readiness* refers to the value of the knowledge and skills in terms of preparation for subsequent courses and grade levels. As teachers rate the importance of standards (step 2 of the process), they can consider these criteria to guide their ratings. For a more formal approach, they might list each standard in a table and check off the criteria that apply to each standard. The majority of instructional time is then spent on the prioritized standards, with other supplemental content being woven into the priority content or taught separately but with less emphasis. We typically recommend that collaborative teams identify between eight and fifteen priority standards for the entire year for a given subject area for a given grade level or course. For example, the following vignettes depict how schools might identify the essential content.

> *Goeling County School District has committed to implementing a guaranteed and viable curriculum. District leaders have selected social studies as the first content area to go through the process and, due to the small size of their district, invited all the social studies teachers to participate.*

continued →

To aid the process, the high school technology department has created an electronic template teachers can use to select prioritized standards. The tool lists all of the state social studies standards for each grade level along with a rating scale. Each teacher independently reads each standard and selects a rating under each of the three criteria—endurance, leverage, and readiness. The electronic form aggregates the responses so the grade-level teams can easily see which standards received high ratings. Members can also identify discrepancies among individuals' ratings of specific standards and resolve them through discussion. Each grade-level team discusses its standards and ratings in order to determine a collective list, which members document on chart paper and electronically.

The next part of the process involves a vertical review of the standards selected by the grade levels (or courses) just above and below each team's level. To do this, the teams hang up their chart paper lists around the room in grade level and course order. During the review, one member of each team stays at the chart to explain their work to others while other team members visit the chart one grade level (or course) above and one grade level (or course) below. For example, the third-grade team reviews second grade and fourth grade. While reviewing the selected standards from the other grade levels or courses, the teachers pose questions and share any concerns about omissions and redundancies. The representative at each team's chart takes those suggestions back to the original grade level or course team for revisions. After a round of revisions based on that feedback, the social studies teams complete one more vertical review. Once the teams finalize their prioritized standards lists, they move on to the development of proficiency scales.

Milert County School District (MCSD) has decided to begin the process of identifying their guaranteed and viable curriculum, starting with ELA and mathematics. MCSD is a large district, so they opt to select a committee of teachers to participate in the process of identifying the most important content. The district leaders send out an application and choose from the interested teachers based on deep-level content expertise as well as an understanding of the state standards and district curriculum documents. They primarily select classroom teachers but also invite instructional coaches, special education and EL teachers, and administrators. In the end, the committee consists of three or four members per grade level for grades K–8, and approximately six members per high school grade level.

The county elects to use a two-day workshop format to complete the process. In addition to Ainsworth's (2003) three criteria, the district also chooses to rate standards based on teacher judgment (as the teachers in the process are content experts) and how much they are emphasized on state assessments. Therefore, on the first day, the teachers learn about five criteria for determining essential content: (1) endurance, (2) leverage, (3) readiness, (4) teacher judgment, and (5) assessment relevance. After gaining understanding of the criteria, the teachers work in grade-level teams to establish an initial list of standards. The next day, the participants gather again for the vertical alignment process. During this process, each team meets with the teams from the grade levels above and below their own to discuss and make changes to the list from the first day of the process. This district plans to use these lists of prioritized ELA and math standards during the upcoming school year as a pilot before conducting the same work in other subject areas.

Including Cognitive and Conative Skills

Creating a guaranteed and viable curriculum is transformational in that it provides teachers with a laser focus regarding the essential content they will teach. Collaborative teams can effect a second transformation in the curriculum by including skills that enable life-long learning. If students are to become college- and career-ready, the PLC process should take into account two categories of such skills: cognitive skills and conative skills (Marzano & Heflebower, 2012). *Cognitive skills* are "those needed to effectively process information and complete tasks" (Marzano et al., 2013, p. 24); *conative skills* involve one's ability to evaluate both information and emotions and then respond or act appropriately (Marzano & Heflebower, 2012). Each category includes specific skills that can be directly taught and used to deepen students' thinking (Marzano et al., 2013). The cognitive and conative skills are reported in tables 3.1 and 3.2, respectively.

Table 3.1: Cognitive Skills

Cognitive Skill	Definition
Generating conclusions	Combining information to create new ideas
Identifying common logical errors	Analyzing conclusions or arguments for validity or truth
Presenting and supporting claims	Using reasons and evidence to support new ideas
Navigating digital sources	Finding relevant information online or in electronic resources and assessing its credibility
Problem solving	Navigating obstacles and limiting conditions to achieve a goal
Decision making	Methodically selecting the best option from among several good alternatives
Experimenting	Generating explanations for events or phenomena and testing the accuracy of those explanations
Investigating	Identifying questions about a topic, event, or idea and discovering answers, solutions, or predictions
Identifying basic relationships between ideas	Understanding and recognizing how two ideas are connected by time, cause, addition, or contrast
Generating and manipulating mental images	Creating images, symbols, or imagined situations in one's mind and using them to test ideas and solutions

Table 3.2: Conative Skills

Conative Skill	Definition
Becoming aware of the power of interpretations	Realizing that feelings, assumptions, and beliefs about a situation affect one's perception of and reaction to it
Cultivating a growth mindset	Understanding that intelligence is not a fixed attribute and that effort can help one overcome challenges
Cultivating resiliency	Developing the ability to redouble one's efforts when faced with a challenge, rather than giving up

Avoiding negative thinking	Preventing emotional reactions or anxiety about the future from controlling one's thoughts and actions
Taking various perspectives	Discovering the reasons and supporting evidence behind various and opposing ideas
Interacting responsibly	Understanding that words and actions influence and affect other people and using effective and assertive communication
Handling controversy and conflict resolution	Combining controversial ideas to come up with a better idea and resolving conflicting ideas or situations in a way that benefits all parties

If collaborative teams have done a good job ensuring that the academic elements of the curriculum are viable, there should be time available to select some cognitive and conative skills to be directly taught along with the academic content. The following vignette depicts how one school emphasized such skills.

> Foudy Middle School has decided to emphasize cognitive and conative skills along with their prioritized content standards. To make sure that students gain experience with a wide range of skills, this focus will be integrated into all subject areas and grade levels. Each collaborative team proposes one or two cognitive and conative skills that its members feel can be well integrated into their content area. Then, the school leaders examine the teams' plans to ensure balance. That is, school leaders check to see if particular skills are being ignored or are receiving too much emphasis. If this is the case, teams might be asked to adjust their focus. A seventh-grade social studies collaborative team wants to help students develop argumentation skills, so those teachers select the cognitive skill of presenting and supporting claims, as well as the conative skill of interacting responsibly. To emphasize these skills, the teachers plan a project that requires students to present well-supported claims and debate with their peers for each unit of study. During the first unit of the year, on Ancient Rome, they assign research and debate projects about whether Julius Caesar was a good or bad leader. To introduce the assignment, they directly teach students how to support claims and interact responsibly. The former involves organizing an argument effectively and knowing what constitutes strong evidence. For the latter, they explore positive discussion practices with their students. In later units, they review this information before students are asked to apply these skills. Once students are proficient with these argumentation skills, the teachers start to incorporate them into informal class discussion as well.

Identifying Learning Goals and Objectives

A third curricular transformation that collaborative teams can undertake is to translate prioritized standards into goals or objectives. The terms *goals* and *objectives* are commonly used interchangeably. We will continue this convention. (For a complete discussion of the use of these and other related terms, see Marzano & Kendall, 2007.) *Objectives* (also known as *goals*) are statements—derived from prioritized standards—that outline the knowledge and skills students need to acquire. An objective should specify a performance, such as "Students will be able to perform long division using remainders" or "Students will be able to correctly identify and name the bones in the human body."

At this stage in the process, objectives need not be extremely specific, but neither should they be too broad. A wide-ranging long-term goal, such as "Students will be able to write a research paper," should be broken down into smaller objectives, such as "Students will be able to identify credible sources and record quotations accurately" and "Students will be able to organize their research papers in a logical manner."

It is important to note that there is a great deal of discussion about the proper way to construct objectives. *Designing & Teaching Learning Goals & Objectives* (Marzano, 2009) addresses this topic in depth. Briefly though, there is no universally accepted way to write objectives. Technically, it is useful to think in terms of two basic forms for an objective.

1. Students will understand _____.

2. Students will be able to _____.

The reason for the two formats is that content knowledge can be organized into two broad categories: declarative and procedural. *Declarative knowledge* is information. One understands information. For example, a student would understand the concept of meiosis. *Procedural knowledge* involves skills, strategies, and processes. A student demonstrates mastery of this type of content by executing the skill, strategy, or process. Therefore, a student would be able to perform the skill of two-column addition. On a cautionary note, we strongly recommend that educators understand these two types of knowledge but not get stuck on how they are stated. In fact, once the distinction is understood, there are many ways to write objectives. As Marzano (2009) stated:

> One final comment should be made about use of the phrases "Students will understand" and "Students will be able to." Some educators object to the use of the verb *understand* in goal statements on the grounds that it is inappropriate and nonspecific. The first part of this criticism is inaccurate. The verb *understand* is entirely appropriate when designing declarative goals. The second part of the criticism is accurate. It is not very specific in that it does not describe how students are to demonstrate their understanding. . . . You will see that we set aside the convention of using the verb *understand* with declarative goals and use more specific verbs such as *describe*, *explain*, and the like. You will also note that we sometimes use the phrase "will be able to" with declarative goals: "Students will be able to explain the defining characteristics of the cell membrane." This relaxing of syntactic rules for stating declarative and procedural goals described is completely appropriate once a teacher has a firm grasp of the distinction between the two types. In the beginning, however, we recommend the use of two different formats to explicitly mark declarative and procedural goals. (p. 16)

In short, there are numerous acceptable ways to phrase objectives for both declarative and procedural content.

Standards statements from state and national documents often include multiple objectives, which should be separated to give the team an accurate idea of how much content there really is. To illustrate the process of generating objectives, consider the following priority standard: "Produce clear and coherent writing in which the development and organization are appropriate to task, purpose, and audience" (National Governors Association Center for Best Practices [NGA] & Council of Chief State School Officers [CCSSO], 2010a, p. 21). Collaborative team members might rewrite this standard as the following objectives.

1. Students will understand task, purpose, and audience.

2. Students will understand why different tasks, purposes, and audiences require different text organizations and styles of writing.

3. Students will be able to develop an idea using various text organizations.

4. Students will be able to match various text organizations to appropriate uses.

As mentioned previously, we typically recommend that collaborative teams identify between eight and fifteen prioritized standards for a year-long course or subject area. Because standards often encompass multiple objectives, the set of prioritized standards might produce around thirty or more individual objectives.

Once a collaborative team has a preliminary list of objectives, teachers can conduct an informal time audit to see if the list is likely to be viable. First, members of the collaborative team calculate the amount of instructional time available. Then, they estimate how much instructional time each objective will consume. Teachers could make these estimates in terms of hours or class periods, which are ultimately equivalent to days of the school year. Teachers then compare the time needed for instruction and the time available for instruction. Many schools have about 180 days of schooling per year. If a team calculated, for example, that it would take 220 days to teach the suggested objectives, it would be clear that they have identified too much content. Teams should also remember that they will devote some instructional time to topics that arise unexpectedly, such as current events. In light of this, teachers may want to allow a buffer of as much as 30 percent of the total instructional time (Marzano, 2003). In other words, the estimated time it will take to teach all of the content in the guaranteed and viable curriculum should be about 70 percent of the total instructional time. If there is too much content, the team should revise their list of essential content by deleting objectives or reclassifying them as supplemental.

Constructing Proficiency Scales

After translating prioritized standards into objectives, a collaborative team can construct proficiency scales. This is the final curricular transformation collaborative teams generate. A proficiency scale organizes identified objectives as a sequence of information and skills—from a simpler learning goal, to the target learning goal, to a more complex learning goal. Stated differently, "Proficiency scales articulate learning progressions for each prioritized standard. Learning progressions describe how students' understanding of a topic develops over time" (Heflebower et al., 2014, p. 26). Figure 3.1 shows the generic form of a proficiency scale.

Score 4.0	More complex learning goal	
	Score 3.5	In addition to score 3.0 performance, partial success at score 4.0 content
Score 3.0	Target learning goal	
	Score 2.5	No major errors or omissions regarding score 2.0 content, and partial success at score 3.0 content
Score 2.0	Simpler learning goal	
	Score 1.5	Partial success at score 2.0 content, but major errors or omissions regarding score 3.0 content
Score 1.0	With help, partial success at score 2.0 content and score 3.0 content	
	Score 0.5	With help, partial success at score 2.0 content, but not at score 3.0 content
Score 0.0	Even with help, no success	

Figure 3.1: Generic proficiency scale.

When creating a proficiency scale, one or more objectives from the standard become the score 3.0 target learning goal. As we have seen, a single priority standard will commonly contain multiple objectives. To illustrate, consider the following standard: "Use informal arguments to establish facts about the angle sum and exterior angle of triangles, about the angles created when parallel lines are cut by a transversal, and the angle-angle criterion for similarity of triangles" (NGA & CCSSO, 2010b, p. 56). This single standard includes the following objectives.

1. Students will be able to use informal mathematical arguments.

2. Students will be able to make generalizations that articulate mathematical principles.

3. Students will understand the angle sum and exterior angles of triangles.

4. Students will understand parallel lines and transversals.

5. Students will understand triangle similarity.

When creating a proficiency scale, team members select one or more of these objectives as the score 3.0 content.

To write score 3.0 learning goals, we recommend that teachers restate or clarify content in the objective to make the scale more useful for planning and instruction. To illustrate, consider the following score 3.0 goal, which is a restatement of several objectives from the prioritized standard.

> Students will be able to use evidence to informally explain relationships among the angles of triangles, including the sum of interior angles and angle-angle similarity.

This restated objective provides more instructional focus and guidance than do the objectives in isolation or the standard from which they were extracted.

As explained by DuFour and Marzano (2011), "The levels of knowledge collaborative teams identify—the target objective, simpler content, and more complex content—are the meat of each proficiency scale" (p. 115). Once the score 3.0 content is in place, collaborative team members create a simpler learning goal by identifying knowledge or skills that are foundational to the target learning goal. The score 2.0 content might be simpler learning goals based on other objectives extracted from the standard, or it might be implicit content that the collaborative team believes is foundational to reaching the score 3.0 content and should therefore be directly taught to students. Simpler learning goals often include vocabulary and basic processes. To illustrate, consider the following score 2.0 content.

> Students will be able to recognize and recall basic vocabulary terms such as *interior angle, exterior angle, angle sum, corresponding angles, congruent,* and *similarity.*

> Students will be able to recognize and recall basic facts such as *the measures of the interior angles of a triangle add up to 180°* and *when two corresponding angles of two triangles are congruent, the triangles are similar.*

Finally, to fill in the score 4.0 content, the collaborative team creates a more complex learning goal by identifying information or skills that go above and beyond the target learning goal. To aid in creating score 4.0 learning goals, teachers can use a taxonomy that describes cognitive complexity, such as Robert J. Marzano and John Kendall's (2007) New Taxonomy, Norman Webb's (2006) Depth of Knowledge, or Lorin W. Anderson and David R. Krathwohl's (2001) revision of Bloom's taxonomy. Such taxonomies organize many of the cognitive skills listed in table 3.1 (page 36) into hierarchic categories. When using a taxonomy, collaborative team members identify the level of rigor of the score 3.0 target learning goal as specified by the taxonomy and then devise a score 4.0 objective based on a higher level of the taxonomy.

To illustrate the use of a taxonomy, consider table 3.3, which depicts the New Taxonomy articulated by Marzano and Kendall (2007). The taxonomy is described in more depth in appendix C (page 139).

Table 3.3: Marzano and Kendall's New Taxonomy

Level of Difficulty	Mental Processes	Terms and Phrases
Level 4: Knowledge Utilization—Applying information or processes in order to complete a larger task	**Decision Making:** Choosing between multiple options	*Decide* *Select the best among the following alternatives* *Which among the following would be best* *What is the best way* *Which of these is most suitable*
	Problem Solving: Overcoming obstacles or limiting conditions to reach a goal	*Solve* *How would you overcome* *Adapt* *Develop a strategy to* *Figure out a way to* *How will you reach your goal under these conditions*
	Experimenting: Generating explanations for a phenomenon and testing the accuracy of those explanations	*Experiment* *Generate and test* *Test the idea that* *What would happen if* *How would you test that* *How would you determine if* *How can this be explained* *Based on the experiment, what can be predicted*
	Investigating: Identifying questions and discovering answers	*Investigate* *Research* *Find out about* *Take a position on* *What are the differing features of* *How did this happen* *Why did this happen* *What would have happened if*

continued →

Level of Difficulty	Mental Processes	Terms and Phrases
Level 3: Analysis— Extending or elaborating on knowledge in a reasoned manner	**Matching:** Identifying similarities and differences	*Categorize* *Compare and contrast* *Differentiate* *Discriminate* *Distinguish* *Sort* *Create an analogy* *Create a metaphor*
	Classifying: Grouping information into categories	*Classify* *Organize* *Sort* *Identify a broader category* *Identify categories* *Identify different types*
	Analyzing Errors: Evaluating the logic and accuracy of knowledge, conclusions, or arguments	*Identify errors* *Identify problems* *Identify issues* *Identify misunderstandings* *Assess* *Critique* *Diagnose* *Evaluate* *Edit* *Revise*
	Generalizing: Inferring broader conclusions from sets of known information	*Generalize* *What conclusions can be drawn* *What inferences can be made* *Create a generalization* *Create a principle* *Create a rule* *Trace the development of* *Form conclusions*
	Specifying: Applying general rules to specific information or new situations	*Make and defend* *Predict* *Judge* *Deduce* *What would have to happen* *Develop an argument for* *Under what conditions*

Level of Difficulty	Mental Processes	Terms and Phrases
Level 2: Comprehension— Understanding and interpreting knowledge such that it can be stored in long-term memory	**Integrating:** Distilling detailed information into a general form and mixing it with prior knowledge	*Describe how or why* *Describe the key parts of* *Describe the effects* *Describe the relationship between* *Explain ways in which* *Paraphrase* *Summarize*
	Symbolizing: Creating nonlinguistic representations of knowledge	*Symbolize* *Depict* *Represent* *Illustrate* *Draw* *Show* *Use models* *Diagram* *Chart*
Level 1: Retrieval— Bringing stored information from long-term memory to working memory	**Recognizing:** Matching given information to stored knowledge	*Recognize (from a list)* *Select (from a list)* *Identify (from a list)* *Determine (if the following statements are true)*
	Recalling: Producing information from long-term memory in response to a given prompt	*Exemplify* *Name* *List* *Label* *State* *Describe* *Identify who* *Describe what* *Identify where* *Identify when*
	Executing: Recalling and carrying out procedural knowledge	*Use* *Demonstrate* *Show* *Make* *Complete* *Draft*

Source: Adapted from Marzano, 2009.

To understand how to use the taxonomy depicted in table 3.3, consider the objective previously identified as the score 3.0 content: *Students will be able to use evidence to informally explain relationships among the angles of triangles, including the sum of interior angles and angle-angle similarity.* It is at the comprehension level (level 2) because it asks students to explain relationships, which falls under the mental process of integrating. To create a score 4.0 objective, the collaborative team moves up to the analysis level (level 3) of the taxonomy. One cognitive operation at the analysis level is comparison. The collaborative team then creates the following score 4.0 objective: *Students will be able to compare the angle sum of triangles to those of other polygons.*

Another approach to score 4.0 is simply to leave the generic description ("In addition to score 3.0 performance, the student demonstrates in-depth inferences and applications that go beyond what was taught") in place, rather than articulating a specific, more complex learning goal. This method communicates that there may be multiple ways a student can demonstrate score 4.0 performance.

With score 2.0, 3.0, and 4.0 objectives articulated, the proficiency scale is complete. This is depicted in figure 3.2.

Score 4.0		Students will be able to compare the angle sum of triangles to those of other polygons.
	Score 3.5	In addition to score 3.0 performance, partial success at score 4.0 content
Score 3.0		Students will be able to use evidence to informally explain relationships among the angles of triangles, including the sum of interior angles and angle-angle similarity.
	Score 2.5	No major errors or omissions regarding score 2.0 content, and partial success at score 3.0 content
Score 2.0		Students will be able to recognize and recall basic vocabulary terms such as *interior angle, exterior angle, angle sum, corresponding angles, congruent,* and *similarity.* Students will be able to recognize and recall basic facts such as *the measures of the interior angles of a triangle add up to 180°* and *when two corresponding angles of two triangles are congruent, the triangles are similar.*
	Score 1.5	Partial success at score 2.0 content, but major errors or omissions regarding score 3.0 content
Score 1.0		With help, partial success at score 2.0 content and score 3.0 content
	Score 0.5	With help, partial success at score 2.0 content, but not at score 3.0 content
Score 0.0		Even with help, no success

Figure 3.2: Completed proficiency scale.

As depicted in figure 3.2, only the score 2.0, score 3.0, and score 4.0 levels contain specific content statements; the rest of the scale describes levels of proficiency by referencing score 2.0, 3.0, and 4.0 content. Score 0.0 indicates no knowledge. Score 0.5 indicates that, with help, the student demonstrates partial understanding of the basic knowledge (score 2.0 content). Score 1.0 indicates that, with help, the student shows partial knowledge of both the simpler learning goal (score 2.0 content) and the target learning goal (score 3.0 content). A student who earns a score 1.5 has independently demonstrated partial knowledge of the simpler learning goal (score 2.0) but made major errors or omissions with the target learning goal (score 3.0). Score 2.0 indicates proficiency with the simpler learning goal. Score 2.5 indicates proficiency with the simpler learning goal and partial understanding of the target learning goal. Score 3.0 indicates proficiency with the target learning goal. To earn a score 3.5, a student must demonstrate proficiency with the target learning goal and partial knowledge of the more complex goal (score 4.0 content). A score 4.0 indicates proficiency with the more complex learning goal.

One question teachers sometimes have about the scale in figure 3.2 is, What does "help" mean? When considering the word *help*, it is important to note that this does not refer to accommodations or modifications articulated in an Individual Education Plan (IEP), a 504 plan, or any other formal documentation. In a proficiency scale, *help* refers to extensive probing questions and prompting by the teacher to discern any proficiency on the student's part at score 2.0 or 3.0. It is not considered help if a teacher simply restates or clarifies a question for a student. On the other hand, if a student requires assistance with many assessment components and demonstrates little to no independence with the content, that student would likely receive a "with help" designation. The following vignette depicts how a teacher might assign a score of 0.5, which indicates partial success at the score 2.0 level with help but no success at the 3.0 level.

> After teaching the mathematics unit titled "Word Problems With Money," Miss Schultz decides to assess the progress of her second-grade students. As the assessment process gets underway, she notices that Jackson seems to be struggling to record anything on his paper. She approaches Jackson and discreetly asks him if he has any questions. He replies, "I don't get what I am supposed to do on this." Jackson has been challenged by this unit of instruction and, as a result, Miss Schultz is not surprised by this current situation. She decides that he needs some reminders in order to demonstrate what he knows on the assessment. She points to the first section on the assessment and says, "Remember the day we played the matching game with coins and value cards?" Jackson smiles and nods his head. Miss Schultz continues, "This part of the test is like what we did that day. Use what we did together to help you on these items." She continues to prompt Jackson, as needed, for the remainder of the test administration. In the end, she is able to discern that he has some knowledge of the content at the 2.0 level and none at the 3.0 level; however, he needed help from her in order to communicate his level of understanding. For these reasons, he receives a score of 0.5 on the assessment.

Student-Friendly Scales

A final step in creating a proficiency scale is to translate it into student-friendly language. Although the proficiency scale is a tool for teachers as they teach, assess, and provide feedback to students, it is also a tool students can use directly. A student-friendly version of the proficiency scale communicates clearly to students what they are expected to know. To illustrate, consider the student-friendly scale in figure 3.3 (page 46), which is based on the scale in figure 3.2. As demonstrated in figure 3.3, student-friendly scales commonly include *I can* or *I know* statements.

Score 4.0		I can compare the sum of the angles of a triangle to the sum of the angles of other shapes, like squares, hexagons, and octagons.
	Score 3.5	I can make connections that weren't directly taught to me, but I'm not always right about those connections.
Score 3.0		I can explain how the interior angles of a triangle and the sum of their measures relate to each other. I can explain why two triangles are similar or not similar based on their angle measures.
	Score 2.5	I know and can do all of the basic content and some of the target content.
Score 2.0		I know what the terms *interior angle*, *exterior angle*, *angle sum*, *corresponding angles*, *congruent*, and *similarity* mean. I know that the angles of a triangle always add up to 180°. I know that similar triangles have to have two angles with the same measure.
	Score 1.5	I know some of the basic content, but I make some mistakes.
Score 1.0		With help, I know some of the basic content and some of the target content.
	Score 0.5	With help, I know some of the basic content.
Score 0.0		Even with help, I don't know any of the content.

Figure 3.3: Student-friendly scale.

Developing Scales One Unit at a Time

Thus far, we have emphasized an approach in which collaborative teams take priority standards and translate them into proficiency scales for the entire year. While this is our recommended method, we have also worked with schools in which collaborative teams create scales one unit at a time. They begin the year by creating a scale or set of scales for the first unit to be taught. Teams also create common assessments based on the scales and track students' progress throughout the unit. This same process occurs before the next unit begins; that is, teams create a scale or scales along with common assessments. This pattern is replicated for the third and subsequent units.

This unit-by-unit approach provides collaborative teams with a gradual introduction to proficiency scales and spreads out the work of scales over the entire year. The main disadvantage of this approach is that collaborative teams do not consider the essential content from a year-long perspective, which requires them to think through how content will be distributed over the whole year. The year-long perspective helps collaborative teams keep in mind the need for a focused set of essential content that progresses over time. This noted, developing scales one unit at a time might be a useful strategy while collaborative teams are adjusting to and developing skill at designing scales. As soon as possible, though, we recommend that collaborative teams develop scales based on the prioritized standards from the perspective of the entire year.

The concept of a guaranteed and viable curriculum necessitates that collaborative teams operate interdependently when identifying what all learners must know and be able to do. When collaborative teams within a school operate in concert, they can design a guaranteed and viable curriculum with accompanying proficiency scales for every subject area at every grade level. The following vignette depicts how one school designed proficiency scales.

Serena Ridge High School is implementing proficiency scales schoolwide. Because this is a new initiative for the school, school leaders have set aside a full day after the school year ends to train teachers and begin writing scales for the following year. During this training, the teachers learn a four-step process.

1. *Identify a standard or objective on which to base the proficiency scale.*

2. *Create the target learning goal by rewriting the standard to explicitly describe what students need to know and be able to do.*

3. *Determine the score 2.0 content by identifying vocabulary and prerequisite knowledge related to the target learning goal.*

4. *Create a score 4.0 learning goal by using a taxonomy of mental processes.*

At first, to practice the concept, the whole group of teachers writes a scale for the same standard. Each teacher performs each step individually, and then the whole group discusses the process and end result before moving to the next stage. Next, teachers split up into their collaborative teams. Each team selects a standard relevant to its grade level or content area and constructs a scale for the standard as a group. Then, each team shares its scale with another team to get feedback. Finally, each teacher writes a scale individually and shares it with his or her collaborative team. Once teachers feel comfortable with the process, collaborative teams spend the rest of the day writing scales that team members will use the following year.

Summary

This chapter has addressed aspects of curriculum that collaborative teams can transform. Specifically, we discussed a number of important elements of curriculum work: identifying essential content, including cognitive and conative skills, translating standards into learning objectives, and organizing the content into proficiency scales. These steps guide teams toward a curriculum that is guaranteed and viable—consistent across teachers and feasible to cover in the time available. In the next chapter, proficiency scales become the basis for a transformation in assessment.

Chapter 3 Comprehension Questions

1. Why is a guaranteed and viable curriculum important?

2. What are the four steps to creating a guaranteed and viable curriculum? Briefly describe each step.

3. Why should standards be translated into learning goals or objectives?

4. Explain each level of a proficiency scale.

Self-Evaluation for Chapter 3

	Strongly Disagree	Disagree	Neither Agree nor Disagree	Agree	Strongly Agree
1. We have identified the essential content.					
2. We have included important cognitive and conative skills.					
3. We have guaranteed that the essential content can be taught in the time available.					
4. We have translated standards into learning goals.					
5. We have organized content into proficiency scales.					
6. We have created student-friendly versions of the scales.					

CHAPTER 4 | Transforming Assessment

Once proficiency scales are in place, a powerful answer becomes possible to the question, How do we know if our students are learning? Indeed, proficiency scales can transform classroom assessments into tools to determine how much students have learned as well as their current status at a particular point in time. There are four concrete steps collaborative teams can take when designing and using assessments based on proficiency scales.

1. Use proficiency scales as the basis for all assessments.

2. Design an assessment blueprint.

3. Write the assessment items.

4. After administering the assessment, score it and discuss the results.

Here we discuss each step in more detail.

Using Proficiency Scales as the Basis for All Assessments

As described in chapter 3 (page 33), a proficiency scale is basically a set of objectives on a specific topic organized into a progression representing their level of difficulty. This makes them the perfect framework from which to design assessments. To illustrate, consider the proficiency scale in figure 4.1 (page 52). In this scale, there are five objectives at score 2.0, one objective at score 3.0, and one objective at score 4.0. Recall from the discussion in chapter 3 (page 33) that some educators prefer to avoid the use of the verb *understand*. We, however, believe it is quite appropriate as long as teams provide more specificity regarding expectations of students elsewhere—for example, in student-friendly scales or instructional activities.

It is not uncommon to design an assessment that addresses all three levels of content in a scale. In such cases, individual items are designed for score 2.0, 3.0, and 4.0 content. This is frequently done with preassessments—those administered before instruction has begun. However, throughout a unit, teams might design one or more assessments that are focused on one level of content only. For example, at the beginning of a unit of instruction, a few assessments might focus only on the score 2.0 content. Later on in the unit, assessments might focus only on score 3.0 content. Here, the teacher assesses students to the level of content that has been explicitly taught in class. If a teacher has only taught the content at the 2.0 level, it might be appropriate to assess only to the 2.0 level. However, some students may be beyond the level at which the teacher has instructed, so providing opportunities for students to demonstrate that understanding may also make sense. Score 4.0 is an example of this. By definition, score 4.0 goes beyond what was explicitly taught, so teachers will commonly include score 4.0 assessment items even though very little instruction has taken place for that level. Score 4.0 assessment items do not count against a student; they provide an opportunity for students to demonstrate a higher level of understanding.

Score 4.0		Students will identify two competing claims about a text, support each with textual evidence, and decide which of the claims is better supported.
	Score 3.5	In addition to score 3.0 performance, partial success at score 4.0 content
Score 3.0		Students will make claims about what a specific text says explicitly and use relevant textual evidence to support those claims.
	Score 2.5	No major errors or omissions regarding score 2.0 content, and partial success at score 3.0 content
Score 2.0		Students will understand the concept of an inference. Students will understand the concept of a claim that is supported by evidence. Students will understand the concept of evidence explicit in a text. Students will find or recognize claims that are supported by textual evidence provided by the teacher. Students will find or recognize textual evidence to support claims provided by the teacher.
	Score 1.5	Partial success at score 2.0 content, but major errors or omissions regarding score 3.0 content
Score 1.0		With help, partial success at score 2.0 content and score 3.0 content
	Score 0.5	With help, partial success at score 2.0 content, but not at score 3.0 content
Score 0.0		Even with help, no success

Figure 4.1: Sample proficiency scale.

Designing an Assessment Blueprint

For each common assessment, the collaborative team creates an *assessment blueprint* (Marzano & Yanoski, 2016), outlining which types of items and how many items there will be on the assessment. To do so effectively, members of the collaborative team must first discuss the content at each level of the scale in order to ensure a strong match between the assessment items and the content. For example, if the content at score 3.0 of a scale addresses students' ability to write an expository essay with special attention to the transitions between paragraphs, assessment items consisting of short-answer and essay questions are more appropriate than a multiple-choice test. Table 4.1 compares four types of assessment items to the proficiency scale levels they are most appropriate for assessing.

Table 4.1: Assessment Item Types and Levels of Knowledge

Types of Assessment Items	Levels of Knowledge		
	Score 2.0	Score 3.0	Score 4.0
	Basic knowledge and skills that students have learned during the instructional unit—fairly easy	More complex knowledge and skills that students have learned during the instructional unit—doable if students were paying attention	Inferences or applications that go beyond what students were explicitly taught—challenging
Forced-Choice Items	Short items with a small number of correct responses; options are often included (for example, multiple choice, matching, alternative choice, true/false, fill-in-the-blank, multiple response [asks for two or more correct answers])		
Short Written Response	Items that require the construction of one to a few sentences		
Essay		Longer written response of several paragraphs; covers more information and often requires students to connect, analyze, or apply information; usually requires students to use multiple levels of knowledge	
Oral Response	Spoken version of forced-choice items or short written responses; longer spoken items such as question-and-answer sessions or structured discussion		

Source: Adapted from Marzano, 2006.

Once the item types are determined, teachers can then consider how many items are needed. It is important that they develop an adequate number of assessment items for each objective in a scale. Each level of the scale will likely have a different number of assessment items associated with it, due to the differing types of content. Score 2.0 assessment items are usually shorter and each cover one or two specific facts or details, so there may be more items at this level than at score 3.0 or 4.0, where each item may cover several aspects of the content and require a longer answer. In general, in a comprehensive assessment, score 2.0 content has five or more items, score 3.0 content has two or more items, and score 4.0 content might only have one or two complex items (Marzano & Yanoski, 2016; Marzano et al., 2013). For example, an assessment might consist of ten multiple-choice questions (score 2.0), three short constructed-response items (score 3.0), and one essay question (score 4.0).

Writing the Assessment Items

Given the preparation described in the preceding sections, the actual writing of an assessment should be relatively straightforward. To illustrate, consider the assessment in figure 4.2 (pages 54–55), which is based on the proficiency scale about making claims in figure 4.1.

SECTION 1

1. When we say that we have made an inference about a text, we mean that we have noticed something that is:
    A. Directly stated
    B. Indirectly hinted at
    C. Explained in a footnote
    D. Not present in the text at all

2. If you are writing an essay about a book and want to support your claim with textual evidence, the best thing to do would be:
    A. Cite a direct quote
    B. Paraphrase the text
    C. Refer to a quote from an expert
    D. Either A or B

3. Consider the following quote from *To Kill a Mockingbird* and then select the claim that it best supports: "Mockingbirds don't do one thing but make music for us to enjoy. They don't eat up people's gardens, don't nest in corncribs, they don't do one thing but sing their hearts out for us. That's why it's a sin to kill a mockingbird" (Lee, 1960, p. 119).
    A. Children are often smarter than adults expect.
    B. Punishing innocent people is wrong.
    C. Some animals are pests.
    D. Always stand up for what you believe in.

4. Consider the following claim about *To Kill a Mockingbird* and select the quote that best supports it: In Maycomb, being masculine or manly means being physically able.
    A. "For some reason Dill had started crying and couldn't stop; quietly at first, then his sobs were heard by several people in the balcony" (Lee, 1960, p. 265).
    B. "Jem grabbed his left wrist and my right wrist, I grabbed my left wrist and Jem's right wrist, we crouched, and Dill sat on our saddle. We raised him and he caught the window sill" (Lee, 1960, p. 70).
    C. "Jem was scarlet. I pulled at his sleeve, and we were followed up the sidewalk by a philippic on our family's moral degeneration, the major premise of which was that half the Finches were in the asylum anyway, but if our mother were living we would not have come to such a state" (Lee, 1960, p. 136).
    D. "Our father didn't do anything. . . . Atticus did not drive a dump-truck for the county, he was not the sheriff, he did not farm, work in a garage, or do anything that could possibly arouse the admiration of anyone" (Lee, 1960, p. 118).

5. Consider the following claim about *To Kill a Mockingbird* and select the quote that best supports it: Women in the story are typically polite on the outside but cruel underneath.
    A. "I wondered at the world of women. . . . I must soon enter this world, where on its surface fragrant ladies rocked slowly, fanned gently, and drank cool water. But I was more at home in my father's world. People like Mr. Heck Tate did not trap you with innocent questions to make fun of you; even Jem was not highly critical unless you said something stupid" (Lee, 1960, pp. 312–313).
    B. "I felt the starched walls of a pink cotton penitentiary closing in on me, and for the second time in my life I thought of running away" (Lee, 1960, p. 182).

C. "When we arrived at the Landing, Aunt Alexandra kissed Uncle Jack, Francis kissed Uncle Jack, Uncle Jimmy shook hands silently with Uncle Jack" (Lee, 1960, p. 107).

D. "Miss Caroline was no more than twenty-one. She had bright auburn hair, pink cheeks, and wore crimson fingernail polish. She also wore high-heeled pumps and a red-and-white-striped dress. She looked and smelled like a peppermint drop" (Lee, 1960, p. 21).

SECTION 2

1. Examine the following three quotes from *To Kill a Mockingbird* and make a claim that is supported by all three. Then, explain how each quote supports your claim.

    "Miss Caroline seemed unaware that the ragged, denim-shirted and floursack-skirted first grade, most of whom had chopped cotton and fed hogs from the time they were able to walk, were immune to imaginative literature" (Lee, 1960, p. 22).

    "In Maycomb, if one went for a walk with no definite purpose in mind, it was correct to believe one's mind incapable of definite purpose" (Lee, 1960, p. 199).

    "[Atticus] did not do the things our schoolmates' fathers did: he never went hunting, he did not play poker or fish or drink or smoke. He sat in the livingroom and read" (Lee, 1960, p. 118).

2. Make a claim about the way most citizens of Maycomb treat children and the way Atticus treats children. Find at least two pieces of textual evidence to support your claim.

3. Make a claim about a theme or point that Harper Lee conveys through the story of Tom Robinson's arrest and trial. Use at least three pieces of textual evidence to support your claim.

SECTION 3

1. Make two opposing claims about a theme, character, relationship, or other situation in *To Kill a Mockingbird*. Support each claim with at least two pieces of textual evidence and then explain which claim is better supported.

Figure 4.2: Sample assessment at three levels.

A key criterion when writing assessment items is *validity*, which means that items measure what they are intended to measure. Using proficiency scales as the basis for writing assessment items helps ensure validity because the scale delineates both the content and its level of difficulty. If a collaborative team uses a proficiency scale to create items based on the content articulated at each level of the scale, each item should address one level of the scale only.

When formatting the assessment as it will be presented to students, we recommend separating 2.0 items, 3.0 items, and 4.0 items into distinct sections of the assessment. This is depicted in figure 4.2—section 1 contains the items for level 2.0 content, section 2 contains the items for level 3.0 content, and section 3 contains the item for level 4.0 content. This will simplify the grading process. If items at different levels are mixed, then teachers must keep track of the difficulty level of each item.

Finally, we should note that designing common assessments based on proficiency scales does not mean that previously constructed assessments need to be discarded. While it is certainly possible that a collaborative team would write entirely original items for an assessment, it is also plausible that they would take items from existing assessments, modifying them as necessary. Teachers can also *backmap* existing assessments by identifying the proficiency scale and level to which each item of an existing assessment relates (for more on backmapping, see Heflebower et al., 2014).

Scoring the Assessment and Discussing the Results

Once students have completed an assessment, the teacher should score it as soon as possible. Typically, scoring is done by individual teachers but it could also be done collaboratively if a team so chooses. It is extremely helpful if, when creating the assessment, a collaborative team also creates a scoring guide for that assessment. Scoring guides are particularly useful for items that are scored using multiple points. For example, items that are assigned five or more points should have a brief description of what type of answer receives a score of 5, what type of answer receives a score of 4, and so on. Tammy Heflebower, Jan K. Hoegh, and Phil Warrick (2014) stated that scoring guides are advantageous because they

> ensure fairness in assessment practices, provide more reliable interpretations of assessment information, and allow for more consistency in . . . scoring. These guides also help each teacher understand which items assess which proficiency level and how to identify correct, partially correct, and incorrect responses. (p. 50)

Teachers can also show scoring guides to students prior to the assessment to clarify the expectations for each level of knowledge.

There are two basic approaches to scoring an assessment that contains items at score 2.0, 3.0, and 4.0 levels of a proficiency scale: (1) using percentage scores at each level, and (2) using response codes at each level. After scoring a common assessment, collaborative teams should convene to analyze the results.

Using Percentage Scores

To illustrate the percentage approach, consider the example in table 4.2.

Table 4.2: The Percentage Approach to Scoring Assessments

Section	Item Number	Possible Points per Item	Obtained Points per Item	Section Percentage
Score 2.0	1	5	5	22/25 = 88%
	2	5	4	
	3	5	3	
	4	5	5	
	5	5	5	
	Total	25	22	
Score 3.0	6	10	7	15/30 = 50%
	7	10	4	
	8	10	4	
	Total	30	15	
Score 4.0	9	10	1	3/20 = 15%
	10	10	2	
	Total	20	3	

The assessment scored in table 4.2 includes ten items—five at the score 2.0 level, three at the score 3.0 level, and two at the score 4.0 level. Each item has a specific number of points that students can possibly earn (third column). The fourth column reports the number of points a specific student earned on each item. The fifth column displays the section percentage, computed by dividing the obtained points by the possible points.

In table 4.2, the student acquired 88 percent of the possible points for the score 2.0 level, 50 percent of the points for the score 3.0 level, and 15 percent of the points for the score 4.0 level. Examining the overall pattern, the teacher then determines how well the student performed overall in reference to the scale. This is done by making decisions about the student's proficiency moving from score 2.0 through score 4.0. The score 2.0 percentage is 88 percent, so the teacher concludes that the student obtained at least a score of 2.0 on the assessment. Next, the student's percentage score for the 3.0 content was 50 percent. The teacher concludes that this is not enough to warrant an overall score of 3.0, but it is enough to warrant a score of 2.5. The teacher stops at this point. If a student has not provided enough evidence to warrant a score at one level, then he or she is not scored at the next level up.

Using Response Codes

With this approach, each student's response on each item is coded as *correct*, *partially correct*, or *incorrect*, as opposed to assigning points to each item. For more specificity, teachers can use *high partial* and *low partial* in place of *partially correct*. After scoring individual items, the teacher determines the pattern of responses and assigns a score accordingly. For example, if a student's answers are correct on all items of the score 2.0 section of the test, partially correct on two items of the score 3.0 section of the test and correct on the third item of the score 3.0 section, and incorrect on the two items of the score 4.0 section of the test, that student would receive a score 2.5 (DuFour & Marzano, 2011). Table 4.3 displays this pattern of responses.

Table 4.3: The Response Codes Approach to Scoring Assessments

Section	Item Number	Correct, Partially Correct, or Incorrect?	Section Pattern
Score 2.0	1	C	Correct
	2	C	
	3	C	
	4	C	
	5	C	
Score 3.0	6	PC	Partially correct
	7	C	
	8	PC	
Score 4.0	9	I	Incorrect
	10	I	
Overall Score			2.5

Source: Adapted from Marzano, 2010.

It is important to note that if the assessment addresses more than one proficiency scale, students will receive one score per scale, rather than one overall score (DuFour & Marzano, 2011). That is, if an assessment includes items that cover two different topics and was designed using two proficiency scales, a student might receive an overall score of 2.5 for one topic and an overall score of 3.0 for the second topic. The teacher does not assign an overall score for the entire test.

Analyzing Results

After giving and scoring an assessment, teachers should discuss the results in a collaborative team meeting. The group might discuss questions such as the following.

- On which parts of the assessment did students perform well?

- On which parts of the assessment did students struggle?

- Were there any patterns evident in the student responses that we should discuss as a team?

- Which students are in need of special attention?

- Does the assessment need revision? Which items? Why?

In the next chapter, we address how answers to questions such as these translate into decisions regarding instructional planning. As indicated by the last question in the list, it may be necessary to revise an assessment for future use. When examining assessment results, it may become clear that a particular item is problematic; for example, if numerous students respond incorrectly on the same score 2.0 item but answer most or all of the 3.0 items correctly, the score 2.0 item should be re-examined. When this is the case, a collaborative team should remove the item or revise it to make it more consistent with the other score 2.0 items.

Using Multiple Types of Assessments

Proficiency scales also provide an opportunity to transform our perceptions of what constitutes an assessment. Technically, *assessments* are "planned or serendipitous activities that provide information about students' understanding and skill in a specific measurement topic" (Marzano, 2006, p. 35). *Measurement*, on the other hand, is the act of translating the information about students gleaned from assessments onto some scale (Marzano, 2006). The use of a proficiency scale as a consistent basis for measurement allows teachers to be flexible in the types of assessments they use. Specifically, there are three broad categories of assessments, all of which are effective means of gathering information about student learning and translating the information to a scale. (For a comprehensive discussion of the three categories of assessments, see Marzano, 2010.) First, there are *obtrusive assessments*, in which instruction stops and assessment occurs. These typically take the form of traditional pencil-and-paper tests like figure 4.2 (page 56), but could also involve oral exams or demonstrations. Second, there are *unobtrusive assessments*, in which instruction or normal classroom activity does not stop, but the teacher observes a student or students and records an assessment score. Often, the students are not aware that they are being observed. The third type of assessment is *student-generated assessments*. With these types of assessments, individual students decide how they will demonstrate a level of proficiency and take responsibility for doing so.

Using all three types of assessments provides teachers with great flexibility. Teachers do not have to administer the same number or the same type of assessments to all students. If a teacher is fairly confident that the common assessments the collaborative team designed accurately represent a specific student's true status on a topic, the teacher might not feel the need to use other forms of assessment. However, if the teacher is not sure that the student's true status on a topic is reflected by the common assessments, the teacher might seek other data points by observing the student in an unobtrusive manner or even asking the student to suggest ways he or she might demonstrate competence.

A New Perspective on Formative Versus Summative Assessments

Marzano (2010) described how proficiency scales provide a unique perspective on the concepts of formative and summative assessment. Typically, we think of summative assessment as a measure of students' statuses at the end of an instructional cycle (such as a unit of instruction). We usually consider formative assessment an ongoing process throughout a learning cycle in which teachers use students' performance on assessments to modify and improve teaching and learning. One misconception still prominent in K–12 education is that the format of an assessment determines whether it is formative or summative. In fact, an assessment is classified as formative or summative depending on how the assessment data are used, rather than on the format of the assessment itself. In other words, teachers could use the same assessment in a formative manner or a summative manner—the teachers in a collaborative team might use the results of a specific obtrusive assessment to assign final scores to students (summative) or to plan and modify future lessons (formative). This is not to say, however, that formative assessments are not scored and recorded. Teachers should score and record assessments for formative use so they can track student progress over time and determine a student's or class's current level of knowledge. From this perspective, proficiency scales and formative assessment are inherently compatible. Proficiency scales provide a detailed, objective progression to which teachers can compare students' current knowledge. The descriptions of each level on the proficiency scale also provide concrete goals so teachers can more easily identify what students need to do or learn to move to the next level.

The preceding discussion also provides a new perspective on how teachers assign summative scores to students. In a traditional system, the final score is often determined by a student's performance on a single summative assessment or by averaging a series of summative scores. Both of these methods are problematic. A score on a final exam may not accurately represent a student's true level of knowledge simply because all assessments contain errors. Averaging test scores is also problematic. Averages assume that a student's level of knowledge has been the same throughout all assessments, which runs contrary to the idea of learning as a progression. Instead, in a formative system, "the teacher examines the student's pattern of responses over time" (Marzano, 2010, p. 28) to assign a summative score. More recent scores receive more weight as they are more reflective of the student's current status than those from the beginning of the learning progression. The summative score may also be influenced by informal instructional feedback rather than being based strictly on formally recorded scores.

Tracking Student Progress

The new view of formative and summative assessment described previously allows for teachers and students to track progress based on proficiency scales. To illustrate, consider figure 4.3 (page 60).

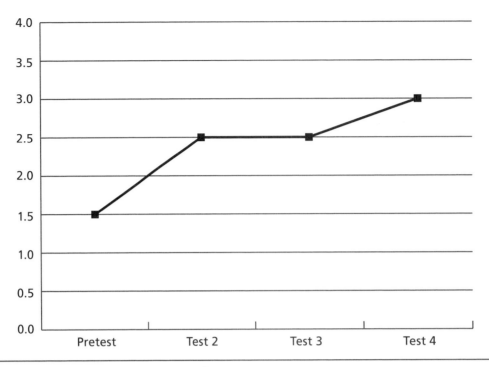

Figure 4.3: Example student progress chart.

Figure 4.3 contains a student's progress chart for a specific proficiency scale used during a particular unit of instruction or a longer learning cycle like a grading period. The unit began with a preassessment that had items for score levels 2.0, 3.0, and 4.0 on the scale. As indicated in figure 4.3, the student's first score was a 1.5, indicating that the student had partial success with score 2.0 and major errors on score 3.0 content. The next score the student attained was 2.5, followed by a second score of 2.5. The final score the student received was a 3.0. This display depicts not only the student's final score of 3.0 but also the student's beginning score of 1.5. Of course, the student's growth is immediately observable—clearly the student has moved from having partial knowledge of the simple content (that is, a 1.5 on the scale) to a final status of understanding the simple content as well as the target content (that is, a score of 3.0 on the scale). The first three scores in the display can be thought of as formative in nature; the final score can be thought of as summative in nature. (For a comprehensive discussion of how student progress can be tracked, see Marzano, 2010.)

A New Vision of SMART Goals

Proficiency scales and assessments based on them increase a collaborative team's ability to track student progress. As a result, teams and schools can more effectively set goals and monitor progress toward those goals. The well-known concept of SMART goals is highly compatible with our model of PLCs. Jan O'Neill and Anne Conzemius (2006) defined SMART goals as (1) strategic and specific, (2) measurable, (3) attainable, (4) results-based (that is, requiring evidence of student learning in order to be achieved), and (5) time-bound. DuFour, DuFour, Eaker, and Many (2010) provided the following examples of traditional SMART goals.

- Our Reality: Last year, 86 percent of the grades assigned to our students were passing grades.

  Our Goal: This year, we will increase the percentage of passing grades to at least 93 percent.

- Our Reality: Last year, 76 percent of our students met the proficiency standards on the state test.

  Our Goal: This year, we will increase the percentage of students meeting the proficiency standards on the state test to 80 percent or higher. (pp. 158–159)

DuFour and Marzano (2011) noted that proficiency scales allow for SMART goals to be much more specific in terms of student learning. They offered the following examples.

By the end of the quarter, 100 percent of students in the class will have gained at least two points on the proficiency scale.

By the end of the quarter, 80 percent of students will be at score value 3.0 or above. (p. 132)

Probably one of the most powerful changes in SMART goals afforded by proficiency scales is that the goals can focus on student growth. For example, the SMART goals listed here focus on growth on the proficiency scale by the end of the quarter.

SMART goals based on proficiency scales can also be more time sensitive. Instead of waiting until the end of the year to ascertain whether they have reached specific goals, collaborative teams can construct meaningful goals that they can accomplish in relatively short periods of time, such as a grading period or even a single unit of instruction. To maximize effectiveness, teams and schools should set both short- and long-term goals. When working toward long-term goals, teachers and school leaders should plan for periodic check-ins to help stay on track and ensure that the ultimate goal will be met.

In all, setting SMART goals creates accountability within teams and schools. Time-sensitive goals focused on student learning can foster a culture of collective responsibility and help teams concentrate on and monitor their work more effectively.

A System of Feedback

Ultimately, the process of transforming curriculum (described in chapter 3, page 33) and assessment (described in this chapter) allows for a system of feedback for both teachers and students. The following points articulate how such a feedback system might manifest through the actions of collaborative teams.

1. **Clear student learning goals are the focus of the guaranteed and viable curriculum.** Collaborative teams develop a guaranteed and viable curriculum in the form of proficiency scales and align them horizontally and vertically throughout the school. Once collaborative teams establish a guaranteed and viable curriculum and articulate proficiency scales, it becomes easy to focus on specific learning goals, as they are explicit in the scales. There is little (if any) individual teacher interpretation as to what should be taught and what should be assessed.

2. **Teachers share learning goals in student-friendly language.** To assist students in understanding what they are learning and what they need to do to demonstrate proficiency, schools change the "teacher-speak" language of learning goals into a student-friendly format. As depicted in chapter 3 (page 33), many student-friendly proficiency scales use *I can* or *I know* statements. Stated differently, "Students cannot assess their own learning or set goals to work toward without a clear vision of the intended learning" (Stiggins, Arter, Chappuis, & Chappuis, 2004, p. 59).

3. **Students set personal goals based on the results of common assessments.** Teachers should share information from common assessments with students to help them see what they have learned and where there are still gaps in their knowledge. Sharing assessment results also ensures that students have the opportunity to reflect on their learning and to provide feedback to the teacher about their results. Though using proficiency scales reduces the variability associated with the validity and reliability of assessment design, it is still critical that students respond to what the assessment indicates to them. For example, if a number of students answer an assessment item incorrectly, teachers can aid the learning process by having students discuss why that happened. Was it a simple mistake? Was it due to a misunderstanding of important content? Can they articulate their mistake or misunderstanding? As part of a formative system, teachers should view assessment as an opportunity for further communication with students, rather than just assigning scores.

4. **Students provide feedback to teachers about proficiency scales and assessment tasks.** If the main aim of collaborative teams is to teach for understanding, then having students examine proficiency scales and assessment tasks for clarification is vitally important. Proficiency scales are meant to provide students with a conception of what they need to learn; therefore, it is critical that students have the opportunity to clarify any misunderstandings or misconceptions with their teachers. Collaborative teams should be willing to refine the language used within a proficiency scale or assessment to make it more accessible to students.

5. **Students celebrate growth in learning.** Students are encouraged and provided opportunities to recognize their own growth and that of others. Teachers might display anonymous progress charts, or classrooms might set up peer recognition systems in which students nominate others for acknowledgement for what they have learned or improved upon. Students may have processing partners, a system in which they explain to their partners what they have learned as a result of working together. This can be very useful when students are analyzing the data from their own assessments. Students can also work together to create learning portfolios or exhibitions in which they specifically discuss how they developed key understandings. The success of such activities hinges on the ability of teachers to promote classroom dialogue both formally and informally.

6. **Teachers promote, encourage, and explicitly teach self-assessment.** As explained by Connie M. Moss and Susan M. Brookhart (2009), "Student self-assessment . . . occurs when students review their own work and identify strengths and weaknesses for the purpose of improving performance" (p. 80). In addition to providing students with feedback, teachers should also provide opportunities for students to self-assess or reflect on their own learning. They should seek to include students in the assessment process. When discussing the results of an assessment, teachers can consider the question, In what ways can we ask students to identify strengths and weaknesses? Reflecting on their own growth can assist students in seeing education not as something that is done *to* them but something over which they have control. This leads to higher levels of self-efficacy. In this way, assessments can motivate students instead of reinforcing a perception that they can or can't succeed in school. Marzano (2006) explained that students need to

perceive that working hard will bring them success. Thus they have a way to succeed, even when faced with challenging tasks. . . . Students who do not believe their efforts produce success can learn over time that they do. (p. 8)

7. **Teachers view information collected from assessments as the students' data, not theirs.** A school operating as a PLC views all information it collects on learning as information that can optimize student growth. The collective norm from which teachers operate is that data from assessments and information about students are intended for students. Collaborative teams work hard to ensure that their collective efforts are shared with students—those who are actually experiencing the learning.

8. **Teachers administer student perception surveys to gather feedback.** A student-centered approach to schooling goes well beyond concerns about academic achievement. Teachers administer surveys to students to gather information about their perceptions of safety, comfort, learning, and their sense of accomplishment and support. Within a collaborative team, staff share the collated results with each other and with students and discuss ways in which identified areas of weakness can be strengthened.

9. **Formal and informal walkthroughs allow school leaders to monitor the school's focus on learning.** At regular intervals, school leaders visit classrooms (sometimes unannounced) and ask questions as a way of eliciting feedback from students. Student feedback is often most honest when it occurs during the natural flow of a school day. Without disrupting instruction, school leaders ask questions related to teaching and learning or more operational aspects of the school, such as, What are you learning about? How are you doing with it? Who do you go to if you are feeling unsafe? What's your favorite time of the day? Why is that?

Changing the Way Student Learning Is Reported

The final transformation regarding assessment that collaborative teams can facilitate is the manner in which schools report student learning. After designing proficiency scales and recording students' formative and summative scores, a natural next step is to apply the scales to grading and reporting practices. In *A Handbook for High Reliability Schools*, Robert J. Marzano, Phil Warrick, and Julia A. Simms (2014) offered the report card depicted in figure 4.4 (pages 64–65). This system is called *standards-referenced reporting* because it reports scores in relation to standardized proficiency scales for specific topics. On this report card, overall grades are reported for subject areas and life skills at the top of the report. A simple translation guide is used to transform scores on proficiency scales into traditional letter grades. To convert proficiency scale scores to letter grades, teachers simply average the summative scores from each proficiency scale and then use the conversion system depicted in table 4.4 (page 66). Proficiency scale scores can also be translated to a 100-point system using the conversion scale in table 4.5 (page 66).

Name:	John Mark	Grade Level:	4
Address:	123 Some Street	Homeroom:	Ms. Smith
City:	Anytown, CO 80000		

Language Arts (LA)	2.46	C	Participation	3.40	A
Mathematics	2.50	B	Work Completion	2.90	B
Science	2.20	C	Behavior	3.40	A
Social Studies	3.10	A	Working in Groups	2.70	B
Art	3.00	A			

		0.5	1.0	1.5	2.0	2.5	3.0	3.5	4.0
LA Reading									
Word Recognition and Vocabulary	2.5								
Reading for Main Idea	1.5								
Literary Analysis	2.0								
LA Writing									
Language Conventions	3.5								
Organization and Focus	2.5								
Research and Technology	1.0								
Evaluation and Revision	2.5								
Writing Applications	3.0								
LA Listening and Speaking									
Comprehension	3.0								
Organization and Delivery	3.0								
Analysis and Evaluation of Oral Media	2.5								
Speaking Applications	2.5								
Life Skills									
Participation	4.0								
Work Completion	3.5								
Behavior	3.5								
Working in Groups	3.0								
Average for Language Arts	**2.46**								

		0.5	1.0	1.5	2.0	2.5	3.0	3.5	4.0
Mathematics									
Number Systems	3.5								
Estimation	3.0								
Addition/Subtraction	2.5								
Multiplication/Division	2.5								
Ratio/Proportion/Percent	1.0								
Life Skills									
Participation	4.0								
Work Completion	2.0								

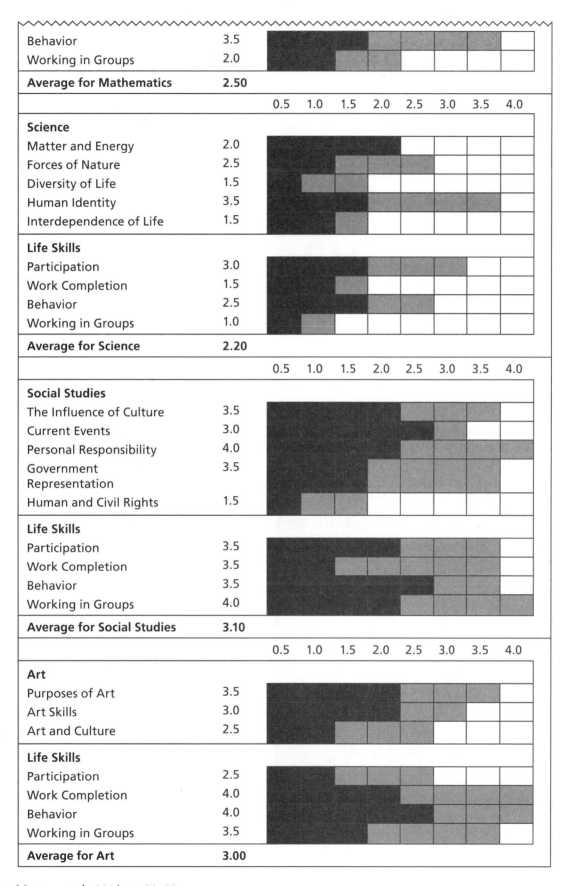

		0.5	1.0	1.5	2.0	2.5	3.0	3.5	4.0
Behavior	3.5								
Working in Groups	2.0								
Average for Mathematics	**2.50**								
Science									
Matter and Energy	2.0								
Forces of Nature	2.5								
Diversity of Life	1.5								
Human Identity	3.5								
Interdependence of Life	1.5								
Life Skills									
Participation	3.0								
Work Completion	1.5								
Behavior	2.5								
Working in Groups	1.0								
Average for Science	**2.20**								
Social Studies									
The Influence of Culture	3.5								
Current Events	3.0								
Personal Responsibility	4.0								
Government Representation	3.5								
Human and Civil Rights	1.5								
Life Skills									
Participation	3.5								
Work Completion	3.5								
Behavior	3.5								
Working in Groups	4.0								
Average for Social Studies	**3.10**								
Art									
Purposes of Art	3.5								
Art Skills	3.0								
Art and Culture	2.5								
Life Skills									
Participation	2.5								
Work Completion	4.0								
Behavior	4.0								
Working in Groups	3.5								
Average for Art	**3.00**								

Source: Marzano et al., 2014, pp. 92–93.

Figure 4.4: Standards-referenced report card.

Table 4.4: Conversion From Proficiency Scale Scores to Letter Grades

Average Proficiency Scale Score	Letter Grade
3.75–4.00	A+
3.26–3.74	A
3.00–3.25	A–
2.84–2.99	B+
2.67–2.83	B
2.50–2.66	B–
2.34–2.49	C+
2.17–2.33	C
2.00–2.16	C–
1.76–1.99	D+
1.26–1.75	D
1.00–1.25	D–
Below 1.00	F

Source: Adapted from Marzano, 2010.

Table 4.5: Conversion From Proficiency Scale Scores to 100-Point Scale

Average Proficiency Scale Score	100-Point Scale Score
4.0	100
3.5	95
3.0	90
2.5	80
2.0	70
1.5	65
1.0	60
Below 1.0	50

Source: Adapted from Marzano, 2010.

In the report card in figure 4.4 (pages 64–65), scores on specific proficiency scales are reported as bar graphs for specific topics (sometimes referred to as measurement topics) within each subject area. The darker portion of each bar indicates the student's level of knowledge at the beginning of the grading period. The more lightly shaded section of each bar shows the student's summative score at the end of the grading period. Consequently, the lighter part of each bar represents a student's knowledge gain. In this way, the report card provides information about both knowledge status and knowledge gain.

Scores for life skills (for example, participation, work completion, behavior, and working in groups) are also reported separately for each subject area and as overall grades in their own right. Each subject area teacher records and reports scores for each life skills topic, and the scores from various subject areas are averaged to come up with overall life skills scores (shown at the top right of the report card). Life skills scores are not combined with academic content scores because—although skills such as working in groups are extremely important—they do not have any bearing on a student's knowledge of specific content. The following vignette depicts how one district transformed their reporting systems.

> Cairn Bridge Public Schools has spent considerable time researching standards-referenced grading and has recently decided to replace their traditional report card with one that gives more precise feedback to students. Through their research, the district has learned that it is important to complete several processes prior to changing the report card, so district leaders develop a plan to ensure success as they transition to the new report card.
>
> First, the district identifies the most important content that all students must master in a grade level or course. Once this content is identified, content experts cluster learning goals into concepts that appear as measurement topics on the report card. For example, in English language arts, the concept of Comprehending Literary and Informational Texts becomes a reporting topic. Teachers also begin using district-level proficiency scales to assess and track student learning. Finally, these shifts are reflected in changes to district report cards. Based on examinations of various types of standards-referenced report cards, the district decides to use a four-point scale similar to the proficiency scale to report learning.
>
> 1 = Student requires help to demonstrate understanding of the learning goal.
>
> 2 = Student is approaching mastery of the learning goal.
>
> 3 = Student demonstrates mastery of the learning goal.
>
> 4 = Student demonstrates performance beyond what was taught.
>
> NT = Not assessed at this time
>
> The district pilots the report card in six elementary schools. During the pilot, stakeholders (including parents) are surveyed to identify any necessary changes. After this initial pilot year, the district implements the new report card in kindergarten through fifth grade and schedules middle and high school implementation for the following two academic years.

Summary

This chapter has addressed the transformation in assessment that a collaborative team can create. Proficiency scales should inform the writing and scoring of assessments. Collaborative teams should adjust their view and use of assessment to create a formative system of feedback. SMART goals can be reconceptualized to focus not only on status, but also on growth. Finally, students' scores should be reported using a standards-referenced system that reports both status and growth. The next chapter discusses the ways in which collaborative teams can transform instruction.

Chapter 4 Comprehension Questions

1. Why are proficiency scales a useful basis from which to create assessments?

2. When creating an assessment blueprint, how many and what types of items are generally appropriate for each level of the proficiency scale?

3. Why should collaborative teams administer common assessments to their students and discuss the results as a group?

4. Identify and describe the three broad types of assessment that can be used to gauge student learning.

Self-Evaluation for Chapter 4

	Strongly Disagree	Disagree	Neither Agree nor Disagree	Agree	Strongly Agree
1. We use proficiency scales as the basis for all assessments.					
2. We write assessment items for each level of the proficiency scale.					
3. We administer common assessments and score them based on the levels of the proficiency scale.					
4. We discuss the results of assessments within the collaborative team.					
5. We use assessments as formative feedback to modify instruction.					
6. We have developed SMART goals based on proficiency scales.					
7. We have students track their own progress.					
8. We report student achievement using a standards-referenced system.					

CHAPTER 5 | Transforming Instruction

The third and fourth questions from table 1.1 on page 4—How will we respond if our students are not learning? and How will we enrich and extend the learning for students who are already proficient?—are both instructional issues. Effective answers to both questions begin with sound planning, which can be enhanced dramatically when conducted in the context of a collaborative team.

Planning

Collaborative teams should conduct two types of planning: (1) planning for high-quality initial instruction, and (2) planning after common assessments.

Planning for High-Quality Initial Instruction

After teachers collaborate to decide upon the critical content to teach (prioritized standards), levels of proficiency (proficiency scales), and the best ways to assess students' understanding (common assessments and assessments used by individual teachers, both based on proficiency scales), it is time to plan for high-quality initial instruction. This initial instructional planning is essential to ensure that all students have the opportunity to learn the content well the first time. Both teachers and students benefit greatly from thoughtfully crafted initial instruction. With thoughtful planning as a backdrop, teachers often report more students obtaining proficiency more quickly. Consequently, teachers need fewer reteaching and reassessment sessions, allowing them to proceed more efficiently and effectively through their prioritized standards (guaranteed and viable curriculum). Students obviously benefit from learning more comprehensively and confidently with sound initial instruction. A very different scenario often occurs when students do not experience high-quality initial instruction. To illustrate, consider the following vignette.

> *Nate is a typical student in ninth-grade algebra. During the initial round of instruction for the first unit of study of the year, his teacher does not clearly define the critical content. She hasn't discussed or planned instructional activities or resources with her colleagues, and therefore teaches straight from the textbook—using only the limited processes and examples given in the text. The teacher proceeds quickly through the content, presenting a great deal of information each day. As a result, Nate makes errors in his thinking throughout this initial instruction. At this point, the teacher administers the common assessment to see how many students have obtained mastery. Nate and over half of the class fail this first assessment miserably. The consequences are dramatic: the students are frustrated at their initial failure, begin to worry that they won't catch up due to the fast pace of instruction, and start to doubt their abilities in algebra, and maybe even in school. Although the teacher might intend to reteach and reassess after analyzing the results of this first assessment, the damage has already been done. The teacher is also frustrated, frantically trying to find time and ways to reteach and reassess over half of the class while simultaneously trying to continue with more new content during class for those students who scored proficiently. Both teachers and students become more and more frustrated, and many capable students are left behind.*

Planning for high-quality initial instruction begins with the levels of the proficiency scales. Specifically, collaborative team members can identify activities and assignments that coincide with score 2.0, 3.0, and 4.0 content on the scale. Heflebower and her colleagues (2014) provided the example in figure 5.1. In figure 5.1, two columns have been added to the proficiency scale. The first additional column contains instructional activities and assignments that can be used to reinforce and review content at score levels 2.0, 3.0, and 4.0. These are things students will be asked to engage in to help develop understanding of and skill with the content in the various score levels of a scale. The second added column contains assessment tasks at each of the three levels. This column does not represent the common assessment that the collaborative team will develop; rather, it provides direction and ideas for the types of assessments individual teachers might design and utilize in addition to the common assessment. These two extra columns can be created by collaborative teams immediately after constructing the proficiency scale itself.

At a more detailed level, collaborative team members can plan for specific lessons based on the proficiency scale. When engaged in such planning, collaborative team members should consider three types of lessons that might be used: (1) direct instruction lessons, (2) practicing and deepening lessons, and (3) knowledge application lessons. Each of these types of lessons involves specific instructional strategies. These are listed in table 5.1 (page 74).

Score	Goal Statement	Instructional Activities and Assignments	Supplemental Assessment Tasks
4.0	The student independently applies place value understanding and rounding to the nearest 10 or 100 in real-world situations.	The student reads real-life examples of using rounding of whole numbers in real-world context. Through teacher-directed discussion, explicit connections are taught and noted.	The student explains how rounding whole numbers to the nearest 10 and 100 helps in figuring a family's grocery bill. The student cites other real-life examples, including explanations of how rounding whole numbers saves time and provides information.
3.0	The student will "use place value understanding to round whole numbers to the nearest 10 or 100" (3.NBT.1; NGA & CCSSO, 2010b, p. 24).	The student will draw three cards from a deck of cards from which the non-number cards have been removed. The student will write down those numbers on a piece of paper to form a three-digit number. He or she will round that three-digit number to the nearest 10 and 100.	The student will solve three-digit place value problems on a pencil-and-paper test. Sample questions include: $900 + 50 + \underline{\quad} = 955$ $3 + \underline{\quad} + 300 = 393$ The student will solve rounding problems on a pencil-and-paper test. Sample questions include: Round 421 to the nearest hundred. Round 956 to the nearest thousand. Please add the rounded numbers from problems 3 and 4 together. The total is \underline{\quad}.
2.0	The student will recognize or recall specific vocabulary, such as *nearest*, *place value*, *round*, and *whole number*. The student will use place value understanding to round whole numbers below 1,000 to the nearest 10 and 100 with visual support.	The student will complete a mix-and-match vocabulary game to review key terms. The student will use visual supports such as pictures to round three-digit numbers to the nearest 10 and 100.	The student will match vocabulary terms to their correct descriptions. The student will match a three-digit number to pictures representing the number rounded to the nearest 10 and 100.

Source: Adapted from Heflebower et al., 2014, p. 56.

Figure 5.1: Proficiency scale with activities and assessment items.

Table 5.1: Instructional Strategies for Different Types of Lessons

Type of Lesson	Strategies
Direct instruction lessons	Chunking content
	Processing content
	Recording and representing content
Practicing and deepening lessons	Structured practice sessions
	Examining similarities and differences
	Examining errors in reasoning
Knowledge application lessons	Engaging students in cognitively complex tasks
	Providing resources and guidance
	Generating and defending claims
All types of lessons	Previewing
	Highlighting critical information
	Reviewing content
	Revising knowledge
	Reflecting on learning
	Purposeful homework
	Elaborating on information
	Organizing students to interact

As the name implies, *direct instruction lessons* involve the teacher presenting content directly to students. Typically, the content is new material that students do not yet know and often includes facts, basic details, and vocabulary. Such content is commonly found at the score 2.0 level in a proficiency scale. Direct instruction lessons might also be needed for content at the score 3.0 level, particularly if that content involves generalizations, principles, or processes that require exemplification and modelling. As depicted in table 5.1, strategies associated with direct instruction include chunking content, processing content, and recording and representing content. These strategies are described in appendix D (page 147). Direct instruction lessons commonly answer the question, How will we respond if our students are not learning?

Practicing and deepening lessons focus on helping students increase the depth of their knowledge or the fluency of their skills. As shown in table 5.1, these lessons might include structured practice sessions, comparisons, or examination of reasoning. These too are described in appendix D. Such strategies are commonly appropriate for score 3.0 content on a proficiency scale. As before, a collaborative team might determine that more practicing and deepening is the appropriate response to the question, How will we respond if our students are not learning? In effect, direct instruction lessons and practicing and deepening lessons are both legitimate responses when students are not learning.

Knowledge application lessons ask students to go beyond what has been taught. They usually address score 4.0 content on a proficiency scale. As shown in table 5.1, knowledge application strategies engage students in cognitively complex tasks, such as experimental inquiry, investigation, and generating and defending claims. These strategies are further explained in appendix D. Knowledge application lessons are commonly the response to the question, How will we enrich and extend the learning for students who are proficient?

In addition to the strategies associated with the three basic types of lessons, all lessons commonly involve instructional strategies that are useful regardless of the level of content being addressed. As depicted in table 5.1, these cross-cutting strategies include previewing, highlighting critical information, reviewing content, revising knowledge, reflecting on learning, purposeful homework, elaborating on information, and organizing students to interact. For example, a teacher could preview new content or highlight critical information in direct instruction, practicing and deepening, or knowledge application lessons. These general-purpose strategies are also described in appendix D.

Determining the type of instructional strategies that might be employed in various lessons that focus on specific levels of a proficiency scale helps teachers in a collaborative team examine the relationship between content and instruction. Some strategies are appropriate for all different types of content; other strategies work best with specific types of content at specific levels of difficulty. In effect, a proficiency scale provides explicit guidance on how to answer the questions:

- How will we respond if our students are not learning?
- How will we enrich and extend the learning for students who are already proficient?

Finally, there are instructional strategies that are not focused on content per se, but are focused on establishing the appropriate context for learning. Specifically, these are strategies teachers can use to engage students, establish rules and procedures, foster good relationships with students, and communicate high expectations for all. These types of strategies help students perceive the classroom as interesting, safe and orderly, nurturing and supporting, and challenging. Strategies to these ends are also described in appendix D.

Planning instructional strategies for specific lessons can and should be a major focus for collaborative teams once proficiency scales have been designed. The form in figure 5.2 (page 76) can be used to facilitate this task. To download a reproducible version of this form, visit **marzanoresearch.com/reproducibles**.

Planning After Common Assessments

In addition to planning for high-quality initial instruction, a collaborative team should assemble and plan right after a common assessment has been administered, whether it is at the beginning of an instructional cycle or in the middle of it. Any time a common assessment is administered, the collaborative team analyzes the assessment results to identify the most pressing needs of students. Of course, this will be different from teacher to teacher. For example, one member of a collaborative team might find that her students are most in need of instruction at the score 2.0 level, whereas another teacher within the team might find that his students are in need of instruction at the score 3.0 level. Collaborative team members could also discuss the instructional strategies that seem warranted given the identified needs of students. For example, direct instruction might be the best approach for the class that demonstrated difficulties with the score 2.0 content, whereas some type of comparison activity may be best for the class with needs at the score 3.0 level.

Additionally, planning after common assessments can be used to group and regroup students. For example, assume that three teachers within a collaborative team are analyzing the results of a common assessment.

What will I do to remind students about the proficiency scale and the specific learning goals we will address today?

What type(s) of lessons will I use in today's class (direct instruction, practicing and deepening, knowledge application)?

What general instructional strategies will I use today?

How will I assess students during the class period?

- Whole-class assessment
- Individual student assessment

What activities will I use to ensure high engagement?

Are there specific students in class to whom I should pay particular attention, and what actions will I take with those students?

- Remind them of rules and procedures
- Actively establish positive relationships
- Actively communicate high expectations

Source: Marzano & Yanoski, 2016, p. 38.

Figure 5.2: Form for lesson planning.

They could identify students who require instruction at the 2.0 level, those who require instruction at the 3.0 level, and those who are ready for score 4.0 activities. The teachers each take responsibility for one group. One teacher takes the score 2.0 students, another takes the score 3.0 students, and the third takes the score 4.0 students. Students would return to their original classes after this specialized instruction occurred.

Figure 5.3 depicts a planning template designed for use after a common assessment. To download a reproducible version of this form, visit **marzanoresearch.com/reproducibles**.

Instructional Approaches	
What specific instructional approaches can we utilize to assist each category of students (listed below) to progress to the next level of learning?	
Significantly Below Proficiency	
On Target for Proficiency	
Already Proficient	
Assessments	
How will we know our instructional approaches have worked? What assessments might we employ to check for understanding?	
Significantly Below Proficiency	
On Target for Proficiency	
Already Proficient	

Figure 5.3: Responding to student needs planning template.

The top part of figure 5.3 focuses on planning for each content level of a proficiency scale. The bottom half of figure 5.3 prompts collaborative teams to identify how they will collect feedback data that will tell them if the strategies they have selected are producing the desired effects.

Lesson Study

Lesson study might be thought of as the ultimate form of collaborative planning. *Lesson study* has been described as "a systematic inquiry into teaching practice . . . carried out by examining lessons" (Fernandez, 2002, p. 394). Best known for its use in Japan, lesson study engages groups of teachers in collaboratively planning a lesson or set of lessons, observing the lessons, and then discussing and modifying them. The process is cyclical and creates continual opportunities for teacher-led professional development. Descriptive studies of the technique almost universally characterize lesson study as a holistic approach that benefits both teachers and students. Teachers are empowered to improve their instructional ability, while students benefit from more effective lessons. One Japanese teacher interviewed by Clea Fernandez (2002) described the experience:

> In my experience lesson study is the most important thing for me to improve my teaching method or teaching techniques. Many teachers have observed me during my lessons and I have asked them to give me comments and to criticize my lessons. . . . Through these experiences, I believe that my teaching method has improved. (p. 395)

Other teachers and researchers (Chokshi & Fernandez, 2004; Fernandez & Chokshi, 2002; Lewis, 1995, 2002a, 2002b; Lewis & Tsuchida, 1998; Stigler & Hiebert, 1999; Yoshida, 1999) have described similar experiences and positive effects of lesson study; some have even ascribed Japan's success in mathematics and science to the use of lesson study (Lewis, Perry, & Hurd, 2004).

It is worth emphasizing that lesson study—when implemented properly—is a significant departure from lesson planning alone and from typical classroom observations. Lesson study is meant to be "a *generative process* through which teachers continually improve and redirect their teaching as needs arise" (Chokshi & Fernandez, 2004, p. 524). The operative word in this description is *continually*; the cycle of lesson study fosters continuous improvement, both in the lesson and in teachers' practice more broadly. Stated differently:

> The experience of engaging in lesson study can inculcate in these teachers a disposition toward continual improvement of their teaching. . . . Lesson study practitioners will obtain even more benefits if they integrate what they learn from their lesson study experiences into their other professional experiences. (Chokshi & Fernandez, 2004, p. 523)

In short, lesson study is a process, rather than a product.

Lesson study can also create a different mindset around classroom observation by providing a nonthreatening environment for teachers to share constructive and detailed feedback about lessons they have planned and observed. In lesson study, the lesson is a collaborative effort, and the group focus makes feedback less critical of individuals.

There are seven steps to the process of lesson study (Fernandez, 2002).

1. Teachers set a goal for their students for the lesson. For our purposes, the goal is a learning goal or objective from a proficiency scale.

2. Teachers come together to plan the lesson as a group. This includes determining the type of lesson (direct instruction, practicing and deepening, or knowledge application) and the specific instructional strategies that will be used to lead to goal attainment. They also create a tangible product of the collaborative planning—a written lesson plan describing the lesson in detail.

3. One of the teachers from the study group teaches the lesson while other group members observe and take careful notes. Observing teachers can also collect data such as narrative records of student learning, what students say and write, and how students use materials.

4. The group convenes and teachers share their observations and reactions to the taught lesson.

5. Teachers create a modified version of the lesson plan.

6. Sometimes, the observed teacher will reteach the lesson with the suggested modifications; other times, a different member of the team will teach the lesson using the modifications suggested.

7. The teacher group observes this modified lesson and shares observations.

Catherine Lewis, Rebecca Perry, and Jacqueline Hurd (2004) identified seven key benefits of lesson study that, combined, lead to instructional improvement.

1. **Increased knowledge of subject matter:** Lesson study requires that teachers discuss content, which naturally raises questions and allows teachers to share knowledge and seek out new information.

2. **Increased knowledge of instruction:** In a manner similar to the increase in content knowledge, lesson study can also increase teachers' pedagogical knowledge as they share ideas and try new instructional strategies.

3. **Increased ability to observe students:** In the lesson study cycle, teachers have more opportunities to observe students and improve their ability to collect data and notice patterns of behavior.

4. **Stronger collegial networks:** The collaborative structure of lesson study helps build community among teachers, especially within a collaborative team. Lewis and her colleagues (2004) explained that "the interpersonal bridges built during lesson study enable collaboration well beyond the research lesson, increasing the coherence and consistency of the learning environment" (p. 20).

5. **Stronger connection of daily practice to long-term goals:** The cyclical process and ongoing nature of lesson study lets teachers monitor student development over time. Additionally, the observational aspect of lesson study allows teachers to notice not only changes in knowledge or assessment scores but also in soft skills like communication and concentration, which are important for students' growth in the long term.

6. **Stronger motivation and sense of efficacy:** Lesson study can help build teachers' desire to improve their practice (Elmore, 2000). Teachers who have participated in lesson study as part of research on the process have experienced that "lesson study puts a professional component back in teaching that is generally missing and treats teaching as a science that teachers can analyze and improve" (Lewis et al., 2004, p. 21).

7. **Improved quality of available lesson plans:** As lessons are tested and revised, their efficacy improves. Using both the experience of the teachers involved and the detailed written lesson plans that result from the lesson study process, these improved lessons can be reused (and possibly further improved) in the future.

On the whole, lesson study benefits teachers because "it honors and professionalizes their work" (Chokshi & Fernandez, 2004, p. 525). More specifically, "lesson study approaches teaching as intellectually demanding work. . . . The attention paid to each lesson honors the importance of teaching as a profoundly complex and interesting endeavor" (Weeks & Stepanek, 2001, p. 4).

The following vignette describes how one school used lesson study.

> *Lloyd Middle School uses an iterative process to engage in lesson study. A mathematics collaborative team has decided to conduct the process on a lesson on probability. First, the team identifies the goal of the lesson: for students to apply their understanding of basic probability theory to real events. This is the score 4.0 content on the related proficiency scale. The teachers spend time discussing what a specific lesson that would guide students to this level of knowledge application might look like. Then, the team moves into more detailed planning. Members focus on how the students would be expected to respond throughout the different parts of the lesson, examining how students might solve a particular real-world probability problem. They also discuss how they will scaffold the lesson to gradually move students to a place where they can independently identify real-world situations in which the principles of probability from the score 2.0 and 3.0 content would apply.*
>
> *After a detailed lesson plan is developed, one teacher conducts the lesson while the rest observe students in the model classroom. Observing teachers record information about how students respond to different elements of the lesson and how they interact with each other and the materials. The focus is not primarily on the teacher, although the observing teachers collect information on how students respond to different questions or comments their teacher poses. After the model lesson, the team debriefs the lesson by sharing their observations. First, the person who taught the lesson shares his or her observations and then other teachers share theirs. Once again, the focus is on the students and whether or not the lesson helped move them toward the goal of real-world content application. Once teachers have shared all their observations, they discuss how the lesson might be modified to better help students meet the learning goal. The team makes a plan to observe the modified lesson in other classrooms.*

Response to Intervention Reconsidered

Although *response to intervention* (RTI)—the academic aspect of overall multitiered systems of support for students—is not formally a component of the PLC movement, it is, in fact, implicitly tied to the implementation of the PLC process. DuFour and Marzano (2011) described the role of RTI in the following way:

> With the passage of the Individuals with Disabilities Education Improvement Act (IDEIA) in 2004, schools and districts were called upon to create a more structured and timely approach to responding to students who experience difficulty in school. This response to intervention (RTI) approach was to be based on high-quality initial instruction for every student in every classroom, continuous monitoring of student learning through formative assessment processes that provided timely information about each student's progress toward desired goals, and tiered systems of intervention that provided extra time and increasingly intensive support for students who continued to struggle. Very importantly, RTI asked educators to take collective responsibility for each student's learning and work collaboratively to ensure that learning. (p. 175)

Clearly, concepts like high-quality initial instruction, continual monitoring, and collective responsibility are inherently compatible with the PLC process. Unfortunately, RTI is not always implemented as intended. DuFour and Marzano (2011) listed a number of mistakes that are commonly made when schools try to implement an RTI system. They include:

- Viewing RTI as an appendage to regular schooling practices
- Viewing RTI as a checklist to complete or a program to purchase
- Viewing RTI as reactive by taking steps only after structures have failed
- Implementing RTI in a way that pulls students out of important learning activities like regular reading instruction
- Focusing on symptoms, like failing language arts, rather than causes like poor decoding skills

The general structure associated with RTI involves three tiers. Tier 1 represents grade-level core instruction. Tier 2 involves supplemental instruction. Tier 3 involves intensive student support. The pyramid in figure 5.4 is commonly used to represent the level of resources focused on each tier.

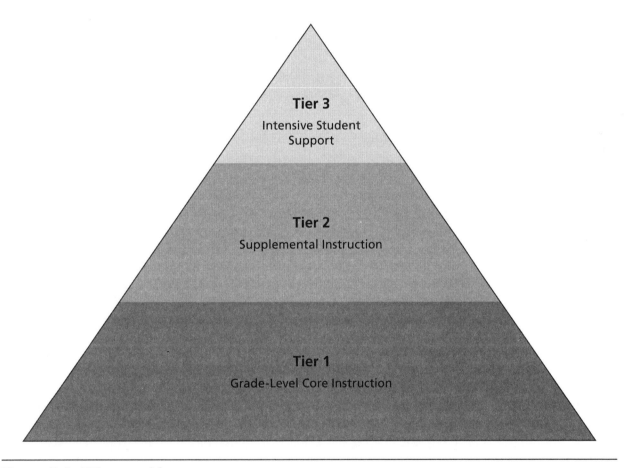

Figure 5.4: RTI pyramid.

As indicated by the size of each tier in figure 5.4, the most robust work will be conducted at Tier 1, which entails designing high-quality initial instruction for every student. Since Tier 1 involves all students, it will certainly require the greatest amount of resources.

Tier 2 is the point at which interventions begin. Specifically, Austin Buffum, Mike Mattos, and Chris Weber (2012) noted:

> Many schools and districts argue endlessly about the language used to define the words *intervention*, *strategy*, and *core instruction*. To bring clarity to the topic, an *intervention* is anything a school does, above and beyond what all students receive, that helps a child

succeed in school. This additional support can be a practice, method, strategy, and/or program. The important consideration is this: if all kids at a school receive it, then it is part of
Tier 1 core instruction and would not be considered an intervention. If a specific practice,
method, strategy, or program *in addition* to core instruction is used on the child's behalf, it is
considered an intervention. (pp. 129–130)

Tier 1 is high-quality initial instruction that ensures all students receive adequate grounding in the score 2.0
and 3.0 content. If high-quality core instruction doesn't work for some students, Tier 2 or Tier 3 interventions
are employed.

The distinction between Tier 2 and Tier 3 interventions sometimes becomes fuzzy, particularly as they
relate to Tier 1 instruction. Buffum and his colleagues (2012) further explained that some schools confuse a
rigid method of placing students in tiers with an effective program of student support:

Rather than create an intervention system that is fluid, flexible, and sensitive to the needs of
each child, schools and districts implement the pyramid as a rigid, protocol-driven program.
Student identification, placement, and duration in each tier are predetermined based upon
screening assessments, cut scores, and program decision protocols. Often, the upper tiers
are disjointed and misaligned to the school's core instruction. School resources and responsibilities are frequently divided, with Tiers 1 and 2 designated for general education and Tier 3
for special education. (p. 11)

When teachers use proficiency scales, the differences between tiers can be well articulated and well coordi-
nated. Where Tier 1 involves high-quality initial instruction for all students regarding content in a scale, Tier
2 interventions are needed for students who are not responding well to the core instruction in score 2.0 and
3.0 content. (Since score 4.0 is going above and beyond what has been defined as proficient, interventions are
not necessary at this level.) Teachers employ Tier 3 interventions when students' academic needs go beyond
the content on the proficiency scale.

To illustrate, assume that the score 2.0 content of a scale includes basic details and terminology about pro-
karyotic cells. A student or group of students who cannot master this content as a result of whole-class instruction would move to Tier 2 intervention. This could be accomplished inside the context of regular classroom
instruction using *small-group instruction* from the teacher—taking those students aside and working with
them in a small group until they become comfortable with the score 2.0 content. Additionally, the teacher
might work with individual students who are having difficulty with score 2.0 content or even pair struggling students with students who have already demonstrated score 3.0 or 4.0 proficiency. Tier 2 interventions
might also involve grouping and regrouping students as discussed previously—three teachers might split up
their students for a class period or two. One teacher would have all the students at the score 2.0 level, another
teacher would have all the students at the score 3.0 level, and the third teacher would have all the students
at the score 4.0 level. When students at the score 2.0 level have demonstrated proficiency with the content,
regular class structure would reassemble. Finally, Tier 2 interventions might also occur outside of the regular classroom. During flexible time periods, small-group and individualized instruction might be offered on
specific topics from specific proficiency scales.

Tier 3 interventions are for those students whose needs go beyond a proficiency scale. For example, some
students might have severe needs regarding basic vocabulary. This would inhibit their ability to progress
through content. Tier 3 intervention would be done outside of regular classroom instruction.

It is important to note that proficiency scales are not designed to address behavioral issues as they relate to multitiered systems of support. On the academic side, however, they do offer a structure that provides new clarity to the RTI process.

Summary

This chapter addressed the transformation in instruction that collaborative teams can create. Planning is an essential part of instruction, one that is improved when done as a team. Teams should create plans to ensure high-quality initial instruction, but should also engage in planning following common assessments to make adjustments to instruction. As part of the instructional cycle, teams can use the lesson study process to improve the execution of specific lessons. Teachers and administrators can also address RTI with more clarity and focus when they use proficiency scales. In the next chapter, we discuss how collaborative teams within a PLC can serve as a vehicle for teacher development.

Chapter 5 Comprehension Questions

1. What are the two types of planning in which collaborative teams should engage?

2. What are the three broad categories of lessons? How do these categories link content to instruction?

3. Describe one way that a collaborative team can respond to student needs identified based on assessment results.

4. Explain the process of lesson study.

5. How do the tiers of RTI relate to the levels of a proficiency scale?

Self-Evaluation for Chapter 5

	Strongly Disagree	Disagree	Neither Agree nor Disagree	Agree	Strongly Agree
1. We plan lessons based on proficiency scales by:					
• Using long-term planning that spans a unit					
• Planning immediately after common assessments					
2. We engage in lesson study.					
3. We use proficiency scales to help plan RTI.					

Transforming Teacher Development

The fifth question in table 1.1 (page 4) is, How will we increase our instructional competence? This is an issue of teacher development. While not commonly mentioned within discussions of the purposes of the PLC process, it has always been an implicit factor.

In a well-functioning PLC, teacher development is not a one-day workshop every few months, nor is it the sole responsibility of administrators to mandate, facilitate, or organize it. Instead, professional development is a continuous, iterative process that members of a collaborative team undertake together. This may initially be uncomfortable for some teachers, as—traditionally—"going public with questions, seeking help from colleagues, and opening up one's classroom to others go against the norms of appropriate teaching behavior" (Cochran-Smith & Lytle, 1993, p. 88). This tradition must change, however. Teacher competence has a well-documented influence on student learning (Marzano, Frontier, & Livingston, 2011; Marzano & Waters, 2009; Nye, Konstantopoulos, & Hedges, 2004); therefore, if the ultimate goal of the PLC process is to improve student learning, improving teachers' instructional prowess should be a major focus of work within a collaborative team. Many theorists and researchers have said as much, focusing on a culture of critical inquiry around teaching (see table 6.1 for examples).

Table 6.1: Inclusion of Teacher Development in Descriptions of PLCs

Source	Description
Louis et al., 1995	Review of a teacher's behavior by colleagues is the norm in the PLC.
Hord, 1997, p. 43	"The democratic professional community allows dissent and debate among its members. . . . Tradition and 'the way we do it here' are challenged and discussed as a means to new insights and practices."
Morrissey, 2000, p. 23	"A critical element in professional learning communities is the continuous engagement of staff in inquiry directed toward improving the learning of students. Such inquiry does not have an endpoint. Instead, it is a state of being, an ongoing process that is sustained over time and changes with the environment and expectations."

continued →

Source	Description
DuFour, 2004	Teachers work in teams to analyze and improve their classroom practice, a key feature of which is the frequent use of formative assessments, which allow for constant investigation, as opposed to solely administering summative assessments.
Timperley et al., 2007	In PLCs, collaboration and collective responsibility for student learning are the norm, rather than individualized, autonomous practice. Teachers plan together, engage in peer observations, and review student responses to analyze the impact of their teaching.
Jackson & Tasker, n.d.	Teachers in PLCs constantly question the status quo. They support one another to try out new methods and learn together from the results, creating innovative solutions to challenges in the classroom.

As noted in table 6.1, improving instruction at the group and individual teacher levels has long been an implicit and explicit aspect of the PLC process. One of the best places to start when attempting to enhance teachers' instructional skills is the use of instructional rounds.

Instructional Rounds

Instructional rounds are not a new idea. In 1982, Judith Warren Little noted that the combination of frequent observation and feedback is one of four factors that are likely to engender the continual professional development of teachers. Many schools use instructional rounds as part of new teacher training or as a way to help less experienced teachers learn from more experienced ones.

Traditionally, when conducting instructional rounds, groups of educators visit the classroom of an effective or expert teacher or the classroom of an instructional coach. This is practical for demonstration purposes; however, as a collaborative team's focus is collaborative improvement, all members of the group should have the opportunity to benefit from observing and being observed by their teammates. Therefore, the group should consider the purpose of the instructional round before initiating each one. If the purpose is to see a teacher model the effective implementation of a strategy, the group should observe an experienced teacher within the collaborative team (or possibly outside it). If the purpose is for a teacher to receive feedback on an aspect of his or her teaching or work toward a goal, the team might observe a less experienced teacher. In either case, the observed teacher should feel comfortable being observed; when the group first starts doing instructional rounds, it may be that not everyone in the group volunteers. After several iterations, however, all teachers should be familiar with the process and become willing to have teammates observe their classrooms.

While some parts of the PLC process (such as proficiency scale development) may be more effectively performed by homogenous content-area or grade-level teams, instructional rounds can be very productive when the group includes a diverse mix of experience, grade levels, and content areas. That is, members from different collaborative teams could be involved in rounds. Teachers with different experiences will naturally notice different things and bring a variety of perspectives to the discussion. We suggest that the ideal number of teachers for a rounds group is between three and six. If there are fewer, it is difficult to have a productive post-observation discussion. If there are more, the observing teachers can become distracting to the observed teacher and his or her students.

When teachers observe one another's classrooms, students often ask what is going on. It is perfectly acceptable to explain to students—in advance or at the start of the observation—that other teachers will be watching part of the class. This lets students know that teachers in the school are working together and learning from each other.

Once an observation begins, the group should stay for fifteen to twenty minutes. This time period provides enough information for discussion without occupying the entire class period. Additionally, these fifteen to twenty minutes do not need to start at the very beginning of the lesson. If the group arrives later (without disrupting the class, of course), they can observe the middle or final minutes of a class instead. If scheduling is a problem, a group of teachers could film a portion of one teacher's lesson and then watch and discuss it later.

Ideally, immediately after the observation ends, the observing group should meet to discuss what they saw. If they cannot meet immediately due to scheduling concerns, the discussion should take place at least within the same day. Groups should expect the discussion to take about twenty-five minutes. In a traditional instructional round, for which the purpose is to learn from an experienced teacher, the observed teacher is not typically included in the debriefing. In the context of the PLC process, depending on the purpose of the round, this may or may not be applicable. All members should have the opportunity to benefit from group discussion, particularly if the purpose of the observation is to give feedback to the observed teacher. For this reason, a collaborative team that observes one of its own members should consider including the observed teacher in the debriefing conversation. If the observed teacher does not participate in the discussion, the observing teachers should plan to provide him or her a summary of a few things the group noticed and discussed productively.

During the debriefing discussion, it is important that teachers link their comments to the purpose of the round. That is, if the purpose is to observe elements of the school's instructional framework, then comments should be related to that topic. If the purpose is feedback, comments should include both positive observations and constructive criticism. All teachers should be expected to contribute to the discussion, because everyone has likely noticed or focused on different things. There can also be a more personal, reflective aspect to the discussion, during which observing teachers might ask questions such as, "How did what I just observed reinforce, validate, or challenge my own instructional practice?" or "Given the example provided by the observed teacher, are there things that I want to consider adding or altering in my instructional practice?"

The following vignettes depict how two schools used instructional rounds.

> *At Vonn High School, instructional rounds serve as a format for teachers to collaborate with their peers and borrow instructional ideas from teachers with whom they may not often interact professionally due to the school's large size. Instructional coaches in the school organize and lead rounds to provide a layer of collaboration focused directly on pedagogy across the entire school. Each teacher is asked to take part in rounds at least once each semester, although they may participate more often if they so desire and spots are available.*
>
> *Teachers in this school sign up to participate in rounds using a shared spreadsheet that displays the days on which rounds will occur and the classrooms that will be observed on each of those days. During the rounds process, two to four teachers, led by an instructional coach, observe instructional practices in two other classrooms for up to fifteen minutes each. Immediately following the rounds, the instructional coach leads the team in a debriefing session. After the debriefing session, the instructional coach sends an email to thank the teachers who were observed. They also provide the observed teachers with feedback regarding instructional practices the rounds participants noticed and want to try in their own classrooms. The following is a sample of an email sent to a teacher who was observed during instructional rounds:*

continued →

Here are some of the amazing practices we saw in your pre-AP biology class-room, which we want to incorporate into our own teaching: you purposely took breaks in instruction to provide opportunities for student questions. Your answers to student questions were clear, focused, and easy to understand. Using models such as "The fat cat ate the rat" to teach gene mutations was a great idea. We were as fascinated as the students when you illustrated gene mutations by changing letters in the sentence.

Instructional rounds at Wooden Elementary School serve as powerful collaborative vehicles for sharing effective instructional practices across the entire teaching staff. At this school, grade-level collaborative teams participate in instructional rounds as a team and observe teachers at other grade levels. As the teams engage in instructional rounds, they record their observations and thoughts on a specific form that is based on the school's model of instruction. This form becomes the basis for the debriefing conversation. The final step in the process occurs when the grade-level teams meet to debrief what they have observed in other classrooms and how they might incorporate new practices into their own work.

Enhancing Reflective Practice

Another method for transforming teacher development is to use the PLC process to foster reflective practice. *Reflective practice* involves deliberate engagement in and reflection on one's own work and abilities. When applying reflective practice to teaching, we suggest a four-step process that is detailed in the book *Becoming a Reflective Teacher* (Marzano, 2012): (1) have a model of effective teaching, (2) set growth goals, (3) engage in focused practice, and (4) receive focused feedback. Teams of teachers can use this process either to work on common goals as a group or to support each other in working on individual goals.

In either case, the first step in the process is to have a model of effective teaching, also known as a language of instruction. By definition, a model of effective teaching delineates those areas a teacher might focus on for reflective practice. While some schools might use their teacher evaluation model or their instructional framework for this purpose, this might not be the best option. Robert J. Marzano and Michael D. Toth (2013) explained that many evaluation models are designed to measure teachers' overall effectiveness as opposed to developing their classroom practice. These are two different purposes and require different approaches. Measurement can be done by examining a teacher's use of a relatively small set of instructional strategies and their direct effect on student learning. Development, on the other hand, requires an examination of a wide array of instructional strategies that allows a teacher to gradually improve his or her instructional prowess.

In chapter 5 (page 71), we provided a rudimentary discussion of our recommended language of instruction. Here, we address that model in more depth. Our recommended model for teacher development, which is based on an updated version of *The Art and Science of Teaching* (Marzano, 2007), is depicted in figure 6.1 and further exemplified in appendix D (page 147).

Feedback

Providing and Communicating Clear Learning Goals

- Providing scales and rubrics
- Tracking student progress
- Celebrating success

Assessment

- Informal assessments of the whole class
- Formal assessments of individual students

Content

Direct Instruction Lessons

- Chunking content
- Processing content
- Recording and representing content

Practicing and Deepening Lessons

- Structured practice sessions
- Examining similarities and differences
- Examining errors in reasoning

Knowledge Application Lessons

- Engaging students in cognitively complex tasks
- Providing resources and guidance
- Generating and defending claims

Strategies That Appear in All Types of Lessons

- Previewing
- Highlighting critical information
- Reviewing content
- Revising knowledge
- Reflecting on learning
- Purposeful homework
- Elaborating on information
- Organizing students to interact

Context

Engagement

- Noticing when students are not engaged and reacting
- Increasing response rates
- Using physical movement
- Maintaining a lively pace
- Demonstrating intensity and enthusiasm
- Presenting unusual information
- Using friendly controversy
- Using academic games
- Providing opportunities for students to talk about themselves
- Motivating and inspiring students

Rules and Procedures

- Establishing rules and procedures
- Organizing the physical layout of the classroom
- Demonstrating withitness
- Acknowledging adherence to rules and procedures
- Acknowledging lack of adherence to rules and procedures

Relationships

- Using verbal and nonverbal behaviors that indicate affection for students
- Understanding students' backgrounds and interests
- Displaying objectivity and control

Communicating High Expectations

- Demonstrating value and respect for reluctant learners
- Asking in-depth questions of reluctant learners
- Probing incorrect answers with reluctant learners

Figure 6.1: A model of effective instruction.

Figure 6.1 contains three major sections: (1) feedback, (2) content, and (3) context. The categories in the feedback section deal with clear goals and assessment relative to those goals. The categories in the content section address the three different types of lessons discussed in chapter 5 (page 71): (1) direct instruction lessons, (2) practicing and deepening lessons, and (3) knowledge application lessons. This section also contains strategies that can appear in all three types of lessons. The categories in the context section address engagement, rules and procedures, relationships, and high expectations. Together these elements provide students with an orderly and affirming environment for learning.

The forty-three elements in this model each contain specific strategies, details about which can be found in the Marzano Compendium of Instructional Strategies (available at **marzanoresearch.com/compendium**). Together the elements in the model encompass over three hundred specific instructional strategies. To illustrate, consider the element titled Increasing Response Rates under the category of Engagement, which is in the context section. There are many instructional strategies a teacher can use to increase response rates, such as wait time, random names, response chaining, voting techniques, and the like. In effect, the model is designed as a resource any teacher can use to select areas on which to engage in reflective practice. Even the most seasoned veteran should be able to find areas of challenge and exploration.

The second step in reflective practice is to set growth goals in relation to the model of effective teaching; this step will vary slightly depending on whether teachers have individual or group goals. In both cases, teachers should begin by performing self-audits of their abilities on each element of the model. Teachers can rate themselves on the elements in appendix D (page 147) on a 0–4 scale, as shown in table 6.2. When teachers rate themselves on an element, they should be thinking in terms of a specific strategy or strategies for that element.

Table 6.2: Reflective Practice Scale

4 Innovating	3 Applying	2 Developing	1 Beginning	0 Not Using
The teacher adapts or creates new versions of the strategy or behavior for unique student needs and situations.	The teacher uses the strategy or behavior and monitors the extent to which it affects student outcomes.	The teacher uses the strategy or behavior but does so in a somewhat mechanistic way.	The teacher uses the strategy or behavior incorrectly or with parts missing.	The teacher should use the strategy or behavior but does not.

Source: Marzano, 2012, p. 37.

After rating themselves on each element of the model, teachers who are setting goals individually can select one or more elements on which they have rated themselves 0 or 1 (that is, Not Using or Beginning) and are interested in improving. In groups that are choosing common goals, each teacher should write the elements on which he or she rated a 0 or 1 on individual slips of paper or sticky notes. Then, the group should categorize the sticky notes, grouping them by element or into related elements. If there are a few elements on which the entire group needs to improve, those would be obvious choices for group goals. Alternatively, the team can vote. Each teacher would receive four stickers or other markers to indicate the elements on which he or she thinks the group should work. The teachers can place these stickers however they like—even all four stickers on one element, if it is particularly important. The element or group of related elements that receives the most votes will be the group's priority goal for the year.

The third step in reflective practice is engaging in focused practice. While engaged in focused practice, teachers keep trying a selected strategy, continually shaping their use of it. This will be a largely individual endeavor whether the group is using individual or common goals. However, a group with common goals might choose a particular element or a specific strategy within an element for everyone to try during the same time period.

The fourth step of reflective practice is receiving focused feedback. This is fairly simple in a team with common goals. Members can observe each other (in person or on video), discuss strategies as a group, and analyze student data as a group. One method for ensuring focused feedback is for each teacher to have a *goal mentor* within the group. For example, if a teacher's goal is to improve his ability to notice and address when students are not engaged, he would pair up with another teacher in the group who (ideally) has a rating of 4 (innovating, the highest score) on the reflective practice scale. This goal mentor would help provide focused feedback to the teacher. Because all teachers have different strengths and weaknesses, each teacher will ideally be able to find a mentor within his or her group and also act as a mentor to others. However, it is possible that a group might have no experts in a particular area and would then ask for help from another collaborative team.

Coaching Through Videos

In the book *Becoming a Reflective Teacher*, Marzano (2012) stated:

> To facilitate the growth process, a teacher needs feedback on his or her use of specific instructional strategies and teacher behaviors related to his or her growth goals. This feedback can come from a variety of sources. One powerful source is video data. (p. 15)

Collaborative teams should set a standing agenda item to give peer feedback for each member's professional growth goals using video recordings. Teams should consider a schedule in which each teacher knows when he or she will be receiving focused feedback from the team regarding his or her selected instructional goals. The teacher then films one or two short segments of him- or herself teaching while using the specific instructional strategy identified in his or her goals. The teacher reviews his or her own video segments individually and notes specific details about the use of the strategy. During the collaborative team meeting, team members view the same video and provide focused feedback to the teacher on the relevant strategy. Ideally, each teacher would receive feedback from at least one peer coaching session during the course of each semester.

Coaching is even more powerful when a collaborative team identifies one or more common strategies. To illustrate, assume the collaborative team has established a common growth goal around the element of previewing new content, and members also decide to use a common strategy for previewing. Specifically, they plan to all use a K-W-L graphic organizer. As an agenda item for their collaborative team meetings, they engage in reflective discussions about their experiences using the strategy in class. Through these discussions, they share ideas and make adjustments to their own personal practice based on feedback from the team. At one point during the semester, each team member video records him- or herself using the K-W-L strategy. During a collaborative team meeting, team members watch the videos and offer focused feedback to each other in the use of the common strategy.

The following vignettes depict how schools might engage in reflective practice.

Reilly High School's world history collaborative team has selected a group focus for reflective practice. Members selected previewing as the instructional element on which to focus because of its importance for the EL students in their classrooms.

As a collaborative team, they initially discuss what each of them has done previously to engage students in previewing new content. Two members of the team have used a K-W-L strategy, but not on a regular basis. One of the members used short video clips to introduce a unit earlier in the year, but he hasn't continued the strategy as a regular part of his practice. After this discussion, each member of the team agrees to research and bring back to the team two examples of previewing strategies they might consider using.

As the team plans instructional units, they deliberately plan and use common previewing strategies in each of their classes. After trying each strategy, the team engages in a group reflective discussion regarding their thoughts on the use of the strategy and the effect of that particular strategy on their students. As a result of the team engaging in reflective practice around the common element of previewing, each teacher expands his or her own practice in this element and, by the end of the semester, acquires several new previewing strategies for his or her own individual practice.

The members of the fifth-grade collaborative team at Whitsell Elementary School have identified student engagement as an issue with which they all struggle. This has been a particular concern during mathematics lessons. In addition to the general sense that students are less engaged during mathematics, student achievement on proficiency scales substantiates the teachers' concerns.

At an earlier meeting, the team decided to try incorporating physical movement into their lessons in an attempt to increase engagement. At their next meeting, they reflect. Data from assessments seem to show that students are retaining more of the content than they had previously. In addition to reviewing data, the team reflects through discussion. Each of the five teachers on the team takes turns responding to a set of questions.

1. *How did I incorporate physical movement into my lessons?*

2. *What did I notice about the use of this strategy during the teaching and learning process?*

3. *What evidence did I collect (perceptual or otherwise) that might indicate the impact this strategy had?*

4. *Where might I rate myself on the reflective practice scale as a result of this focus?*

The group then synthesized its thinking by asking the following inquiry-based collaborative questions.

- *What might we be learning as a result of implementing this strategy?*

- *How might we apply this to other learning experiences for our students?*

The group agrees that physical movement has been helpful in increasing student engagement during math lessons. Now that members feel more comfortable using this strategy, they plan to continue using it during math lessons and try it out in other subject areas.

Student Feedback

Direct feedback from students can be a powerful tool in transforming teacher development. Feedback includes not only achievement data but also the opinions and impressions of students, such as those gathered through student surveys. Unfortunately, student feedback or "pupil voice" (Bolam et al., 2005, p. vi) is often left out of discussions of the PLC process. Clearly, if the ultimate goal is to improve student learning, student voice should play a role in the PLC process. There are a number of questions teachers can ask to solicit feedback from their students. Figure 6.2 (page 96) depicts some questions we have used with schools across the United States. The twenty-one questions in figure 6.2 provide a rather robust picture of students' perceptions within a specific class. We commonly recommend that teachers initially survey a class with whom they feel like they are connecting well. Later on, they might select a group of students with whom they are not connecting well and compare the results.

The scale of each of the twenty-one questions can be quite revealing. The scale spans from *strongly disagree* to *strongly agree* with *neither agree nor disagree* as the center point. Obviously, a response of *strongly disagree* or *disagree* indicates students do not perceive that their teacher has a specific trait or produces the specific results articulated in an item; conversely, responses of *agree* and *strongly agree* indicate that students perceive that a teacher does possess a specific trait or produce a specific outcome. Additionally, a student response of *neither agree nor disagree* provides very useful information for a classroom teacher. To illustrate, consider the item "I am motivated to learn in this class." If a significant number of students respond neutrally to this item, it is probably an indication of an area in which the teacher might want to improve. Certainly a teacher would want the vast majority of students, if not all, to respond that they agree or strongly agree to statements such as this one. Collaborative team members might decide to administer small sets of items from the survey in figure 6.2 (a reproducible version of which is available at **marzanoresearch.com/reproducibles**) and compare their results.

Action Research

A final activity we recommend for enhancing professional development is for teachers to engage in action research. Unfortunately, education research often has a bad reputation among teachers, as such information has sometimes "been used to blame teachers for the failings of the larger educational and sociopolitical systems" (Cochran-Smith & Lytle, 1993, p. 88). While it is true that educators must occasionally embrace negative data from outside researchers (DuFour, 2004), research conducted *by* teachers can be both empowering and extremely helpful toward the goals of the PLC process, as Cochran-Smith and Lytle (1993) note:

> There is little disagreement that teachers who engage in self-directed inquiry into their own work in classrooms find the process intellectually satisfying; they testify to the power of their own research to help them better understand and ultimately to transform their teaching practices. (pp. 18–19)

Many researchers have proposed promising methods to help teachers use data to examine the effectiveness of their instruction (Gallimore, Ermeling, Saunders, & Goldenberg, 2009; Jaquith & McLaughlin, 2010; Means, Padilla, & Gallagher, 2010). While quite sound, these techniques require a certain level of expertise in statistical analysis techniques. While acquiring such knowledge and skills is certainly worth the effort, many teachers have difficulty finding the time and resources to master the requisite competencies.

	Strongly Disagree	Disagree	Neither Agree nor Disagree	Agree	Strongly Agree
1. The teacher of this class is fair.					
2. The teacher of this class cares about me.					
3. The teacher recognizes me for my successes in this class.					
4. I am motivated to learn in this class.					
5. The teacher does not tolerate inappropriate behavior in this class.					
6. I feel safe in this class.					
7. I have many friends in this class.					
8. The teacher in this class keeps reminding us what is most important to learn.					
9. I know what the teacher expects of me in this class.					
10. Students in this class are generally respectful of each other.					
11. The teacher regularly lets me know how I am doing.					
12. The teacher of this class grades me fairly.					
13. The teacher encourages me to learn as much as I can in this class.					
14. The teacher makes lessons interesting in this class.					
15. I try very hard to understand what is being taught in this class.					
16. I have done my best work in this class.					
17. The teacher of this class encourages me to do my best.					
18. The teacher doesn't let students give up when the work gets hard.					
19. I actively participate in this classroom's discussions.					
20. I enjoy the work I do in this class.					
21. I pay attention when I am in this class.					

Figure 6.2: Student feedback questions.

In an effort to facilitate teachers' understanding and use of research methodologies, Trudy L. Cherasaro, Marianne L. Reale, Mark Haystead, and Robert J. Marzano (2015) developed the instructional improvement cycle and the tools necessary to implement it. The improvement cycle and the accompanying toolkit were developed by Regional Education Laboratory (REL) Central at Marzano Research in partnership with educators from York Public Schools in Nebraska. This is a free public domain resource that can be found at **relcentral.org**. As described by Cherasaro and her colleagues (2015):

> In York Public Schools, as part of teachers' professional development experiences, teachers are asked to independently evaluate instructional strategies by identifying two classes with similar instructional units and then teaching one class using an innovative instructional strategy (experimental group) and the other class using customary instruction (comparison group). Teachers collect pre- and post-test data using teacher-developed assessments to evaluate whether the instructional strategy appears to work well.
>
> Regional Educational Laboratory (REL) Central collaborated with York Public Schools to create protocols and tools for these teachers that could be self-executed without the need for external data analysis. (p. 1)

The instructional improvement cycle has four recurring phases: (1) select an instructional strategy, (2) implement the strategy, (3) collect data on strategy implementation, and (4) analyze the data and reflect on the results (see figure 6.3).

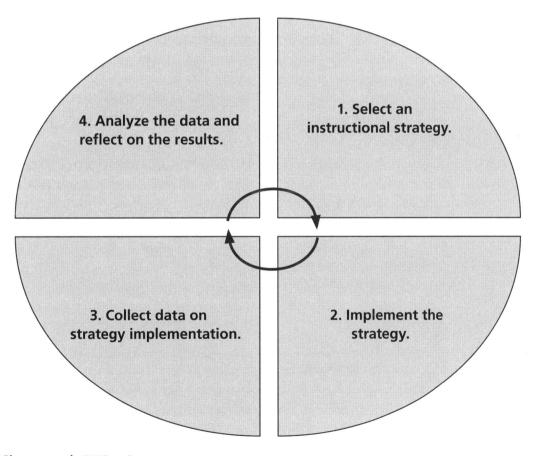

Source: Cherasaro et al., 2015, p. 2.

Figure 6.3: Instructional improvement cycle.

Teachers can implement the instructional improvement cycle over the course of a single unit that is being taught to two different groups of students. Teachers select an instructional strategy (perhaps from the model of effective teaching in appendix D, page 147) and implement the strategy with one group of students but not with the other. The same pretest and posttest are administered to both groups. The only difference between how instruction manifests is that one group receives the instructional strategy and the other does not. Both groups should be instructed by the same teacher and be similar in beginning knowledge status and other factors. In scientific research, researchers select experimental groups (those that receive the strategy) and control groups (those that do not receive the strategy) at random for rigor. As this is not practical in a classroom environment, teachers should compare two similar classes of students.

Cherasaro and her colleagues offered the following example of how one teacher used the process:

> A grade 9 English language arts teacher is interested in learning whether the use of nonlinguistic representations (for example, graphic organizers or concept maps) during vocabulary instruction will help increase student achievement. The teacher implements a nonlinguistic representation strategy in fourth-period English class (experimental group) and uses regular instruction during sixth-period English class (comparison group). Both classes have upcoming lessons with focused vocabulary time, with the learning goal that students can identify prefixes, roots, and suffixes to determine meanings of words. The teacher administered a previously developed vocabulary quiz to both groups of students as the pre-test before implementing the nonlinguistic representation strategy. The teacher administers the same quiz at the end of the two-week unit as the post-test. (p. 3)

The complete approach developed by Cherasaro and her colleagues has three tools that aid teachers in carrying out the four phases of the instructional improvement cycle: (1) the planning guide, (2) the Excel analysis tool, and (3) the reflection guide. The planning guide walks teachers through the first three phases of the instructional improvement cycle: (1) selecting an instructional strategy, (2) implementing the strategy, and (3) collecting data on strategy implementation. The Excel analysis tool also enables the third phase (data collection), while the reflection guide applies to the fourth phase (reflecting on results).

The Excel tool is perhaps the most unique aspect of the entire system in that it provides teachers with immediate, sophisticated statistical analyses with simple data entry. Based on the pretest results, the Excel tool tells teachers whether there is *baseline equivalence*—enough pre-existing similarity in achievement between the two groups to draw reasonable conclusions. Once posttest data have been entered, the tool calculates an *effect size*, a standardized measure of "how much better or worse on average the students in the group that received the strategy did compared with students in the group that did not receive the strategy" (Cherasaro et al., 2015, p. 4). Finally, the tool determines the *confidence* level, which suggests whether one can expect similar results in other classes.

To illustrate the nature of the Excel analysis tool, consider figures 6.4 and 6.5 (page 100). Figure 6.4 displays the data entry portion of the tool. The first column contains student ID numbers. The second and third columns contain the pre- and posttest data from the experimental group (that is, the group that received the instructional strategy). The fourth and fifth columns contain pre- and posttest data for the comparison group (the group that did not receive the strategy). Once a teacher has entered these data, the Excel analysis tool computes the results (as exemplified by figure 6.5). The first results column (baseline equivalence) tells you whether the experimental and comparison groups were equivalent to begin with. The next column tells you whether or not confidence can be placed in the effect size, and the final column reports the actual effect size. Although the term *effect size* is not frequently used by classroom teachers, it is an important piece of information for teachers engaged in action research. As Cherasaro and her colleagues (2015) noted:

	Student Data			
Directions	Keep a list of the students that you assign to each ID to align their pre- and posttest data	Type in pretest percent-correct data (that is, the number of points earned or questions correct divided by the number of points or questions possible) for Control and Experimental Groups		Type in posttest percent-correct data (that is, the number of points earned or questions correct divided by the number of points or questions possible) for Control and Experimental Groups	
	Student ID	**Pre-Experimental**	**Post-Experimental**	**Pre-Comparison**	**Post-Comparison**
	1	23	57	21	57
	2	24	64	21	64
	3	25	89	34	89
	4	26	99	54	99
	5	27	100	37	100
	6	28	24	66	24
	7	28	35	23	35
	8	29	36	29	36
	9	30	57	30	57
	10				
	11				
	12				
	13				
	14				
	15				
	16				
	17				
	18				
	19				
	20				
	21				
	22				

Source: Cherasaro et al., 2015, p. 14.

Figure 6.4: Data entry in the Excel analysis tool.

The effect size (last box on the results screen) compares the scores on average from the comparison and experimental groups to show how much larger (or smaller) the average score is in the class where your new strategy was used compared with a class where it was not used. A positive effect size means that the students who received the strategy did better on average, while a negative effect size means that the students who did not receive the strategy did better on average. The larger the effect size, the larger the difference between the groups. For example, an effect size of 0.50 indicates a larger effect than an effect size of 0.01. (p. 15)

The third tool in the toolkit is the reflection guide. It is designed to help teachers examine the results of their study in such a way as to improve their instructional practices, as well as plan and conduct more studies in a rigorous and useful manner. The first section of the reflection tool asks teachers to consider their results—whether or not there was confidence in the effect size and whether the effect size was positive or negative. The second and third sections, respectively, have teachers reflect on their implementation of the strategy and the characteristics of their assessments. Finally, the last section of the reflection guide helps teachers plan their next steps.

Results		
Baseline equivalence determines whether groups had significant differences in achievement before you implemented your strategy.	The confidence is the certainity of the effect related to an estimate of the range of the effect size if repeated samples were taken. If the range crosses zero there is not much certainty that this effect would hold true in other samples.	Effect size shows differences in average scores between the comparison and experimental group.
Is there baseline equivalence?	**Confidence in the effect size?**	**Effect Size**
No—Select different groups for comparison	**No**	−0.01
Refer to the reflection guide for additional information about how to interpret the results.		

Source: Cherasaro et al., 2015, p. 14.

Figure 6.5: Results in the Excel analysis tool.

The instructional improvement cycle and its three related tools provide collaborative teams with opportunities to engage in action research projects never before available to teachers with any degree of ease or rigor. It is a powerful toolkit that creates new opportunities for research conducted by classroom teachers.

Summary

This chapter has addressed transformations in teacher development that collaborative teams can achieve. Specifically, teams can use instructional rounds, engage in reflective practice, gather student feedback, and do action research. Having covered the work of collaborative teams themselves in this and the previous three chapters, we use the final chapter of this book to discuss the role of school leaders in the PLC process.

Chapter 6 Comprehension Questions

1. Why are collaborative teams an appropriate and effective forum for teacher development?

2. Describe the process of instructional rounds. What purposes can this process serve?

3. How can a collaborative team implement reflective practice?

4. What is the role of student feedback in a PLC? How can teachers obtain student feedback?

5. What is action research? What are its benefits?

Self-Evaluation for Chapter 6

	Strongly Disagree	Disagree	Neither Agree nor Disagree	Agree	Strongly Agree
1. Professional development is ongoing.					
2. We use instructional rounds to:					
• Give feedback to colleagues and team members					
• Learn by observing expert teachers					
3. In our use of reflective practice:					
• We have a model of effective teaching					
• We set individual and/or group growth goals					
4. We engage in team coaching using video recordings.					
5. We acquire student feedback and modify our teaching based on the results.					
6. We engage in action research.					

CHAPTER 7 | # Transformative Leadership

The sixth question in table 1.1 (page 4) is, How will we coordinate our efforts as a school? This is a leadership issue. It is important to note that this chapter is titled differently from previous chapters. Specifically, previous chapters have started with the gerund *transforming* (that is, transforming curriculum, transforming assessment, transforming instruction, and transforming teacher development). The message in those chapters was that the PLC process, when conducted in the manner described in this book, will help transform curriculum, assessment, instruction, and teacher development. The PLC process is the agent of these transformative changes. This chapter is titled "Transformative Leadership." The implication here is that leadership is the agent in transforming the PLC process as described in this book, which, in turn, can transform curriculum, assessment, instruction, and teacher development. This makes intuitive sense. Strong leadership is required to effect the changes described in previous chapters.

The Importance of School Leadership

Discussions of how to improve schools have always pointed to the importance of leadership. However, the specific leadership behaviors that help schools improve were not well known until the late 1990s. Indeed, Robert Donmoyer (1985) noted, "Recent studies of schools invariably identify the principal as a significant factor in a school's success. Unfortunately these studies provide only limited insights into how principals contribute to their school's achievement" (p. 31). Since Donmoyer's comments in 1985, a number of studies have been conducted to identify the specific behaviors principals might engage in to increase their schools' effectiveness. These include studies by Philip Hallinger and Ronald H. Heck (1998), Kathleen Cotton (2003), Kenneth Leithwood, Karen Seashore Louis, Stephen Anderson, and Kyla Wahlstrom (2004), Robert J. Marzano, Timothy Waters, and Brian A. McNulty (2005), and the Wallace Foundation (2013).

None of these reviews specifically addressed leadership in the context of the PLC process. In 2011, however, DuFour and Marzano took the framework created from the Marzano et al. (2005) study and applied it to schools that were aspiring to become PLCs. We have further adapted the DuFour and Marzano model to focus specifically on collaborative teams. This most recent adaptation is presented in table 7.1 (pages 104–105).

Table 7.1: Leadership Behaviors in the PLC Process

Principal Responsibility	Application to Collaborative Teams
1. Providing affirmation and celebration of staff effort and achievement	Using the goals of each collaborative team to recognize and celebrate progress toward those goals
2. Challenging the status quo as a change agent	Knowing the work in which each collaborative team is currently engaged and interacting with them in a way that challenges members to go beyond their expectations
3. Establishing processes to ensure effective communication throughout the school	Ensuring that each collaborative team has easy access to school leaders during and outside of meeting times
4. Recognizing and rewarding accomplishments of collaborative teams and individuals within these teams	Keeping track of the extent to which collaborative teams and individuals within them accomplish their SMART goals and acknowledging those accomplishments
5. Shaping the assumptions, beliefs, expectations, and habits that constitute the school's culture	Establishing and promoting schoolwide norms regarding collaboration in teams and the purpose of collaboration
6. Protecting teachers from outside distraction	Ensuring that the times set aside for collaborative teams are protected and ensuring the collaborative time is used for its intended purposes
7. Demonstrating flexibility in meeting the different needs of teams and being willing to make modifications to school procedures	Recognizing the most appropriate and effective type of guidance and support that is required for individual collaborative teams and executing that necessary behavior
8. Focusing on clear goals and relentlessly pursuing the school's purpose and priorities	Ensuring that each collaborative team has identified and is working toward clear goals that can only be achieved if members work interdependently to achieve them
9. Articulating the ideals and beliefs that drive the day-to-day work of the school	Systematically interacting with collaborative teams from the perspective of schoolwide ideals and beliefs
10. Soliciting input from staff in the design and implementation of procedures and policies	Empowering collaborative teams to make important decisions that directly impact the quality of student learning and regularly seeking input from teams regarding schoolwide decisions
11. Engaging staff in the ongoing review and discussion of the most promising practices for improving student learning	Sharing relevant research and theory with collaborative teams and engaging them in action research regarding the instructional strategies that directly impact student learning
12. Participating in the design and implementation of curriculum, instruction, and assessment	Clarifying the work of collaborative teams, monitoring that work, and engaging in dialogue with teams regarding curriculum, instruction, and assessment
13. Demonstrating interest in and knowledge of curriculum, instruction, and assessment	Providing collaborative teams with ready access to information on promising practices in curriculum, instruction, and assessment, and learning with team members as they apply that knowledge
14. Creating processes to provide ongoing monitoring of the school's practices and their effect on student learning	Monitoring the individual and aggregate impact of the efforts of collaborative teams on student achievement, engagement, and perceptions, and providing teams with the tools to monitor their own progress

15. Creating the conditions that optimize school improvement efforts	Using evidence of student learning and positive peer pressure within collaborative teams to inspire teachers to explore new practices
16. Establishing clear procedures and orderly routines	Establishing clear expectations and protocols for the work of collaborative teams
17. Serving as a spokesperson and advocate for the school and linking staff to external resources	Connecting collaborative teams to resources and support outside the school
18. Establishing a positive working relationship with teachers and staff	Using collaborative teams to increase accessibility to teachers and become more familiar with individual teachers and their concerns
19. Providing teachers with the time, resources, materials, and support to help them succeed at what they are being asked to do	Ensuring that each collaborative team has the necessary materials, information, and support to effectively execute their work
20. Recognizing the undercurrents of the informal organization of the school and using that information to be proactive in addressing problems and concerns	Using ongoing discussions with collaborative teams to discern current or future issues that might affect the functioning of the school
21. Being visible throughout the school and having positive interactions with staff and students	Meeting with each collaborative team on at least a quarterly basis and being actively involved in their concerns

Source: Adapted from DuFour & Marzano, 2011.

As illustrated in table 7.1, the twenty-one leadership responsibilities are easily redefined in terms of the PLC process in general and their specific application to collaborative teams. In effect, table 7.1 provides a blueprint for leadership that works through the collaborative teams as opposed to individual teachers. School leadership can be accomplished much more efficiently and effectively if conducted through the vehicle of collaborative teams. That is, as depicted in table 7.1, the school leader uses his or her interaction with collaborative teams (as opposed to individual teachers) to effect change.

Second-Order Change

In addition to the general findings on school leadership summarized in table 7.1, Marzano and his colleagues (2005) found that leadership looks different if a school is involved in second-order change as opposed to first-order change. *First-order change* refers to small, incremental changes that do not ask stakeholders to make substantial shifts in their thinking. *Second-order change*, on the other hand, "alters the system in fundamental ways, offering a dramatic shift in direction and requiring new ways of thinking and acting" (Marzano et al., 2005, p. 66). Various theorists have described these two levels of change. For example, Ronald Heifetz (1994) described these changes in the context of types of problems. Type I problems are familiar and can be solved using tried-and-true methods. Type II problems may require creative problem solving but are still manageable within traditional ways of thinking. These first two types relate to first-order change, while Type III problems—those that traditional paradigms cannot solve—relate to second-order change. Chris Argyris and Donald A. Schön (1974, 1978) describe this dichotomy in terms of single-loop and double-loop learning. In the case of single-loop learning, a person or group facing a problem tries various strategies that have worked in the past until they find one that solves the problem. Problems that require double-loop learning cannot be solved by existing strategies, so innovative strategies or new perspectives are required.

Many of the innovations described in previous chapters might constitute second-order change in a school. For example, the concept and process of creating proficiency scales as described in chapter 3 (page 33) might constitute second-order change, as might the new ways of designing and scoring assessments described in chapter 4 (page 51). The new approaches to instructional planning and instructional rounds described in chapter 5 (page 71) might be second-order change in a school, as might the approaches to teacher reflection or action research described in chapter 6 (page 87).

Leadership for Second-Order Change

Marzano and his colleagues (2005) found that seven of the twenty-one responsibilities reported in table 7.1 (pages 104–105) were critical to second-order change. This is not to say that the other fourteen are unimportant. Rather, when collaborative teams are charged with changes that are second order in nature, seven responsibilities must receive special attention and be redefined to a certain extent. Here, we consider each of these seven key responsibilities in the context of specific second-order changes that might occur in a school.

1. **Demonstrating interest in and knowledge of curriculum, instruction, and assessment:** In the context of second-order change, responsibility 13 focuses on being knowledgeable about how the innovation will affect curricular, instructional, and assessment practices and providing conceptual guidance in these areas. To illustrate, consider the innovation of creating report cards like the one depicted in figure 4.4 (pages 64–65). That report card includes traditional A, B, C, D, F grades, but it also reports each student's current status and growth from the beginning of the grading period using bar graphs. This type of report card would constitute a second-order change in many, if not most, schools throughout the United States. To execute this responsibility, a school leader must study how the new report cards will affect the curriculum, instruction, and assessment. The innovation will require that the curriculum be not only guaranteed and viable but also articulated as proficiency scales that allow for the tracking of individual student progress. Teachers conduct instruction in such a way as to allow students to work on topics previously addressed in class in an effort to raise their previous scores on proficiency scales. Finally, the assessment system must allow for a variety of types of assessment that staff members can employ at any time for individual students. The leader must consider all of these eventualities.

2. **Creating the conditions that optimize school improvement efforts:** In the context of second-order change, responsibility 15 must focus on being the driving force behind the innovation and fostering the belief that it can produce exceptional results if members of the staff are willing to apply themselves. To illustrate, consider the innovation of teachers setting personal growth goals for their pedagogical skill as described in chapter 5 (page 71). In a school where there is no history of such behavior, the school leader must be the driving force behind the initiative—in effect, be its personal sponsor. This would include behaviors such as attending all professional development activities related to the innovation, setting his or her own personal growth goals, and interacting with teachers about their personal growth goals while visiting collaborative teams.

3. **Engaging staff in ongoing review and discussion of the most promising practices for improving student learning:** In the context of second-order change, responsibility 11 focuses on being knowledgeable about the research and theory regarding the innovation and fostering

such knowledge among staff through reading and discussion. To illustrate, consider the innovation of proficiency scales discussed in chapters 3 and 4 (pages 33 and 51, respectively). To fulfill this responsibility relative to this innovation, the school leader would have to supply staff members with information about proficiency scales that captures their imagination and interests. Such information would surely include research about the innovation, but it also might involve position papers relative to the issue. Teachers would be invited to try out proficiency scales to determine their utility. Some teachers might even be intrigued enough to engage in action research as described in chapter 6 (page 87).

4. **Challenging the status quo as a change agent:** In the context of second-order change, responsibility 2 focuses on challenging the status quo and being willing to move forward on the innovation without a guarantee of success. To illustrate, consider the innovation of instructional rounds discussed in chapter 6 (page 87). To address this responsibility, the leader might collect data on the extent to which teachers have previously had opportunities to observe other teachers. Such data might make the point that teachers generally work in isolation. The leader would encourage discussion and debate about the need for instructional rounds, as well as the process for conducting them. The leader would firmly assert that, as a part of the PLC process, volunteer collaborative teams would at least try implementing instructional rounds as a means of stimulating professional growth and sharing ideas.

5. **Creating processes to provide ongoing monitoring of the school's practices and their effect on student learning:** In the context of second-order change, responsibility 14 must focus on continually monitoring the impact of the innovation. To illustrate, consider the innovation of establishing priority standards as described in chapter 3 (page 33). To execute this responsibility, the leader would collect data on the extent to which the priority standards that were identified truly represent a viable curriculum—one that could be taught in the time available. The leader would also collect data regarding the extent to which teachers use the priority standards as the basis for the taught curriculum. Finally, the leader would monitor teachers' reactions to the new focus on the guaranteed content.

6. **Demonstrating flexibility in meeting the different needs of teams and being willing to make modifications to school procedures:** In the context of second-order change, responsibility 7 focuses on being both directive and nondirective relative to the innovation as the situation warrants. To illustrate, consider the innovation of lesson study described in chapter 5 (page 71). As collaborative teams craft their common lessons and observe their execution, they might experience disagreement on how the target lesson should be changed. To execute this responsibility, the leader would have to balance staying out of the discussion (being nondirective) with guiding the discussion to alleviate discord (being directive).

7. **Articulating the ideals and beliefs that drive the day-to-day work of the school:** In the context of second-order change, responsibility 9 focuses on the leader operating in a manner consistent with his or her ideals and beliefs relative to the innovation. To illustrate, consider the innovation of identifying cognitive and conative skills as part of the guaranteed and viable curriculum as described in chapter 3 (page 33). It would be an obvious inconsistency for a leader to support the direct teaching of conative strategies for responsibly and respectfully clearing up conflict to students without requiring the same behavior of staff and faculty. Similarly, it would be an obvious inconsistency if a leader were to support the direct teaching

of the cognitive skill of providing evidence for one's claims without requiring the same of faculty and staff.

As explained previously, all twenty-one responsibilities are important aspects of regular school management. However, second-order change requires an emphasis on the seven responsibilities described here.

Flattening the Organization

The type of leadership described in the preceding sections cannot be accomplished by an individual charismatic leader. When school or district leaders dispense school-improvement directives, they often fail to "garner ownership, commitment, or even clarity about the nature of the reforms" (Fullan, 2007, p. 11). Marzano and Waters (2009) explained that leaders can use the concept of defined autonomy to strike a balance between being too controlling and too lenient. *Defined autonomy* refers to a strategy in which the leader sets general boundaries and goals but allows latitude and personal choice within those boundaries. This style has also been called "simultaneous loose-tight leadership" by DuFour, DuFour, Eaker, and Many (2010, p. 208). Such strategies allow leaders to provide the necessary vision for key school goals and initiatives yet provide opportunities for collaborative teams to engage in multiple leadership functions. Allowing collaborative teams to participate in the leadership process helps distribute leadership and flatten the organization. The following vignette depicts how one school with which we have worked approached this issue.

> As a way to flatten its leadership structure, Catamount High School established the Learning Leadership Team (LLT), a concept articulated by Michael Fullan (2008). The LLT serves as a campus-based "think tank" to underscore the idea that learning is the work of the school. Faculty, staff, and school leaders, as well as students, engage in this work. The structure of the team was purposely developed to serve as a formal venue for staff input and to provide transparency in decision making for the entire faculty. The permanent membership of the LLT consists of all campus administrators, the department head for each curriculum department, and the lead guidance counselor. Additionally, "open chairs" are available to any teacher from any department who wants to participate in the meeting. To fill the open chairs for their department, interested teachers simply notify the department chairperson. Teachers filling the open chairs are provided opportunities for input and can offer suggestions on any topic being considered by the LLT. In essence, an open-chair team member is treated and expected to participate as any permanent member of the team.

As another example, the following vignette exemplifies how two districts used similar structures to involve various stakeholders in the leadership process.

> Although one is located in Nebraska and the other in Wyoming, two districts have enacted very similar processes in that both districts have identified a "curriculum council" that holds a high degree of responsibility. Each council is made up of approximately forty-five educators, including the superintendent, principals, assistant principals, instructional coaches, collaborative team leaders, and teacher leaders. These individuals have assumed responsibility for important work, such as curriculum

articulation, proficiency scale development, assessment development, and so on. A key responsibility of group members is learning through professional development opportunities. These learning opportunities often result in a product of some sort (for example, curriculum maps, proficiency scales, assessments, or instructional units). In addition to the learning and development components, curriculum council members are responsible for ensuring that other educators in the district are provided with the information learned during professional development. Teachers are also provided with any products the council develops and are given an opportunity to provide feedback and suggest revisions.

Both of these curriculum council processes include ten to twelve professional development days per year for the council members. Additionally, each calendar year includes two or three days for whole-staff collaboration. Additional collaboration occurs during collaborative team meetings. In one district, this time consists of an early dismissal one day per week, allowing about seventy-five minutes for productive work time. The other uses common planning time for collaboration.

Some Lessons We Have Learned

Collectively, we have worked with schools in all fifty of the United States and most of the states in Australia, as well as many other countries. Through these experiences, we have learned a great deal about what to do, as well as what not to do. Here we consider some of the ways that the PLC process can go awry.

Neglecting to Address Misunderstandings About Collaboration

The most common pitfall is for an administrator to assume that collaborative teams understand the concept of collaboration and the work they must complete as a result of their collaboration. As we have seen, collaborative teams should focus on issues of curriculum, assessment, instruction, and self-development—all aimed at enhancing student achievement. While one might think this is obvious, a common issue with newly formed collaborative teams is a lack of clear understanding of the work they are expected to complete. Administrators need to clearly communicate the work that is to be done and monitor that work through the collection of artifacts produced by collaborative teams. Each collaborative team meeting should have a concrete focus on some aspect of curriculum, assessment, planning, or personal development that is specific, concrete, and definable.

Failing to Be Flexible With Teachers of Electives

Another common mistake administrators make in the PLC process is how they deal with teachers who teach electives. These individuals may be the only teachers of a specific content area in the school. We addressed this issue briefly in chapter 2 (page 17); here we elaborate on that earlier discussion. Regardless of the size of the school, elective teachers often find themselves in structures that don't seem to fit cleanly with the nature of their content. For example, a vocal music instructor may be the only such teacher in the school and find it hard to design common formative assessments or even talk about any specific curriculum offerings with other teachers. Administrators can remedy this by altering the expectations for the collaborative process with these teams and clarifying that some teams may take a slightly different approach than a team collaborating in a like subject area. Consider the following three examples that reflect common realities in many schools.

For the first example, consider a school that has one teacher for art, one teacher for vocal music, and one teacher for instrumental music. Each of these three teachers would most likely be teaching multiple courses within their area of expertise. In a case such as this, school administrators need to provide some direction with regard to how this team's collaborative goals may be a bit different than those of a core subject team. This in no way means their work is less effective or important. One option is to have these teachers collaborate around the goal of incorporating literacy skills, such as writing, into each of their courses. This provides a common focus on writing in the content area, and the collaborative team now has a common set of skills that cross each discipline. As part of this collaborative work, the team could explore and develop a common proficiency scale that they will use for assessing writing samples from their students. Through the use of the common scale, the collaborative team can develop a common assessment, collect writing samples from their students, exchange samples within the team, and cross-score papers to enhance the reliability of their scores. If writing is not the cross-disciplinary focus, specific cognitive or conative skills might assume the same role.

As a second example, a collaborative team consisting of teachers from various career and technology education courses might collaborate to develop a set of goals for students in the area of personal finance, since this topic can fit into any of their courses. As a result, the collaborative team develops a set of minilessons to build financial literacy with their students. The collaborative team can practice the concept of common assessment by incorporating one or two common items into their otherwise different assessments. These items would be specifically directed at connections to financial literacy from the minilesson they planned collaboratively and taught within their own specific courses.

As a third example, consider a school that has three physical education teachers who each teach a different level or course in the physical education curriculum. This team might be asked to collaborate in the development of the vertical curriculum and identify how they will chunk and teach the concept of healthy lifestyles at different levels of the curriculum. Essentially, the team is planning for the spiraling of knowledge as students progress through the different levels of physical education. As part of their collaborative process, the team could develop assessments that will be used at each level to measure student knowledge retention as they move from one level to the next in this content area. These assessments would provide data the team can use to see if students are retaining the essential knowledge and skills the team has identified at each level.

Ignoring Teachers Who Will Not Collaborate

A final mistake we have often seen administrators make is ignoring teachers who purposefully avoid the collaborative process. Again, we addressed this briefly in chapter 2 (page 17). Administrators must react and get involved when collaborative teams are not functioning well, or they risk damaging the entire culture of collaboration in the school. DuFour and Marzano (2011) addressed this: "Leaders who are unwilling to confront staff members who ignore the collaborative team process not only undermine that process, but also damage their relational trust with the rest of the faculty" (p. 86). Addressing these issues may be as simple as giving a reminder of the importance of collaborative time; however, corrective actions may also involve some hard conversations. Jennifer Abrams (2009) suggested conversation scripts as a technique for difficult conversations:

The most foundational pieces of a "good start" for a hard conversation include the following:

- Setting the tone and purpose of the conversation
- Getting to the point and naming it professionally
- Giving specific examples
- Describing the effect of this behavior on the school or colleagues or students
- Sharing your willingness to resolve the issue and have a dialogue and discussion

Write out these segments or pieces of the script as though you are completing a rough draft. Writing the words down will help you be sure you have all the parts. Once you are done writing, it is essential to read your script aloud to hear how it sounds. (p. 64)

Appendix B (page 125) includes further guidelines for challenging conversations.

Confronting counterproductive behavior is essential because, ultimately, behaviors that aren't challenged are accepted. However, it is also important to remember that, just as some students need more time to learn, some teachers will need additional time and support in the adjustment to a PLC system. School leaders should seek to support their staff in this process. Questions that leaders can ask include the following.

- What avenues do staff have to seek support when experiencing difficulty?
- What professional learning opportunities have been provided to team leaders to deal with difficult team members?
- How can we ensure we are communicating with team leaders on an ongoing basis?
- What perceptual data might we collect to identify areas of concern and misunderstanding among staff?
- In what ways are we monitoring the effectiveness of the norms and discussion protocols being adopted by teams?
- How might we model the type of learning-centered behavior we want to see in our school?

Addressing questions such as these helps administrators make fewer assumptions about the implementation of the PLC process in their schools. Asking teachers about their experiences is one of the simplest yet most underutilized tools for keeping the PLC process on track. Issues and misperceptions are much easier to correct when leaders have a clear picture of the problem at hand.

Where to Start?

From the discussion in this chapter and previous chapters, it is evident that initiating and sustaining the PLC process is a complex and labor-intensive endeavor. A leader faced with such a daunting task might rightfully ask, "Where do we begin?" Our collective answer is to support the collaborative process. Figure 7.1 (page 112) contains some suggestions regarding this issue. To download a reproducible version of this checklist, visit **marzanoresearch.com/reproducibles**.

Preliminary Processes

☐ Establish and train a leadership team that includes key teacher leaders and is responsible for the school's overall vision.

☐ Identify specific collaborative team structures the school will use.

☐ Establish the frequency with which different teams will meet.

☐ Adjust the schedule to provide collaborative time.

☐ Develop internal (for staff) and external (for students and parents) communication regarding the collaborative team process.

☐ As a leadership team, model the collaborative process expected from teams schoolwide.

☐ Survey staff beliefs, understandings, and experiences regarding collaboration.

Beginning Schoolwide Collaboration

☐ Communicate clear expectations for the work in which collaborative teams will engage, such as creating proficiency scales or developing teacher abilities.

☐ Facilitate the creation of group norms by distributing samples, collecting copies of each team's norms, and providing feedback to teams regarding those norms.

☐ Identify and collect specific artifacts or products from collaborative teams to monitor their initial work and provide feedback.

☐ Develop a sit-in schedule to observe the collaborative process of each team.

☐ Highlight best practices and celebrate the work of collaborative teams that are functioning well.

☐ Periodically ask collaborative teams to engage in self-evaluation regarding adherence to team norms.

☐ Meet with the leadership team to reflect on initial progress and plan support needed for continued progress.

Continuing Schoolwide Collaboration

☐ Continue to collect artifacts of practice to monitor the work of all teams.

☐ During staff meetings, have various collaborative teams present products of their work.

☐ Identify and assist teams that are struggling with the collaborative process.

☐ Intervene and take necessary action for teams that are dysfunctional or not engaging in the collaborative process.

☐ Focus sit-in observations on teams needing the most assistance and provide more autonomy to teams functioning well.

☐ Meet with the leadership team to reflect on the schoolwide collaborative team processes and plan for adjustments if necessary.

Figure 7.1: Checklist for establishing and maintaining collaborative teams schoolwide.

Figure 7.1 contains three sections: (1) preliminary processes, (2) beginning schoolwide collaboration, and (3) continuing schoolwide collaboration. The first set of suggestions addresses the preliminary work that lays the foundation for the work of collaborative teams. It involves making decisions about processes and structures and determining teacher and staff readiness for collaborative work. The second section contains suggestions regarding support of and interaction with newly formed collaborative teams. It involves specific actions and protocols that communicate the message that collaboration is valued and will be sustained throughout the year. The third section contains suggestions regarding those behaviors that are required to sustain effective collaboration within the school. It involves strategies for fostering inter-team communication and addressing problems that have arisen or are likely to arise.

The suggestions in figure 7.1, when enacted effectively, should ensure that the collaborative process as described in chapter 2 (page 17) functions well and is sustained. Given this foundation, the issues of curriculum, assessment, instruction, and teacher development described in chapters 3 through 6 become the concrete work in which collaborative teams engage. The concept of the guaranteed and viable curriculum as described in chapter 3 (page 33) should probably be the first order of business. When this is established, the design and implementation of assessments as described in chapter 4 (page 51) will come naturally. Somewhat simultaneous with the focus on assessment is the focus on planning for effective instruction as described in chapter 5 (page 71). Finally, teacher development, as described in chapter 6 (page 87), can begin at any point, even during the initial stages of developing collaborative teams.

Summary

In this chapter, we explored the type of leadership that drives the PLC process. While collaborative teams have the ability to transform many aspects of education, it is difficult for them to do so without focused, transformational support from school leaders. Leaders of a school attempting the PLC process must focus on specific leadership attributes that enable substantial change. In addition, we suggested that some leadership responsibilities be distributed to collaborative teams. Finally, we revisited the creation of collaborative teams through the lens of common mistakes and provided guidance on where to start in the PLC process.

Chapter 7 Comprehension Questions

1. Describe the importance of effective leadership to the PLC process.

2. What is second-order change?

3. How does leadership for second-order change differ from leadership for more basic changes?

4. What does it mean to "distribute leadership" or "flatten an organization"? Why is this important in a PLC?

Epilogue

In this book, we sought to provide a clear picture of the PLC process and the work of collaborative teams. Although the concepts of professional collaboration and PLCs have been extant in literature and practice for many years, there has been a notable lack of practical guidelines for educators who wish to undertake collaboration. We have endeavored to remedy that situation.

To start, teachers and school leaders must establish schoolwide and team-specific structural and cultural foundations for collaboration. With this groundwork in place, collaborative teams should begin curriculum work, which includes identifying priority content, writing objectives, and constructing proficiency scales. Based on proficiency scales, teachers in collaborative teams can create and administer common assessments and analyze the results. Proficiency scales and the combined resources of collaborative teams can also transform instruction, especially when planning for high-quality initial instruction and planning after common assessments are a regular part of collaborative work. Additionally, collaborative teams are an ideal forum for ongoing, embedded professional development. Finally, this entire process is driven by support and leadership at the school and district levels. The model we have presented here is a practical, holistic approach to teacher collaboration that can transform schools to the benefit of teachers and students.

The subtitle to this book is *The Next Step in PLCs*. Throughout the chapters, we have attempted to articulate what this means and how to do it. As a group, we firmly believe that the PLC process is on the cusp of a breakthrough in its effect on student learning. This will occur if earlier visions of the PLC process are expanded to include the innovations in curriculum, assessment, instruction, and teacher development that we have described. Our hope is that this book makes that next step an easier step for schools to take than it would be otherwise.

APPENDIX A

Answers to Comprehension Questions

Chapter 2 Comprehension Questions

1. **Why are schoolwide norms important?**

    Schoolwide norms are important because the entire school operates as a PLC. To create consistency of purpose and execution across the various collaborative teams, the whole school community should be tied together by schoolwide norms.

2. **Identify three structures that should be allowed for in a PLC schedule. What are common ways that schools make time for these structures?**

    The most essential scheduled structure is collaborative time for teams to meet and work together. Other structures include regular intervention time and meetings between school leaders and collaborative teams. Many schools make time for collaboration by scheduling a common planning period for team members. Others use late-start or early-out schedules for students to create opportunities for teacher collaboration. Intervention time could be scheduled on a schoolwide basis by periodically setting aside instructional time; intervention could also be handled within a collaborative team by grouping and regrouping students within the team. Collaborative teams' meetings with school leaders can easily be accomplished by having leaders attend portions of team meetings or by having collaborative team representatives meet with the leader at another available time.

3. **Describe two common structures for collaborative teams. What are the pros and cons of each?**

    Two frequently used groupings for collaborative teams are grade-level teams and subject-area teams. Grade-level teams are often able to serve a common set of students in a cross-curricular manner, consider broad pedagogical topics, and create opportunities for interdisciplinary learning. On the other hand, subject-area teams can focus closely on the specifics of their content area, such as common assessments and curriculum design within and across courses.

4. **Explain the importance of the following three aspects of collaborative team culture and give an example of how a team might establish and monitor each one.**

    A. Group norms

        Group norms are essential for governing team interactions and work. They operate as guidelines for respectful discussions and sometimes define the type of work that the team will engage in. A team can establish norms by brainstorming as a group and narrowing down the list through discussion or voting. Monitoring adherence to the norms is as simple as periodically surveying team members.

    B. Trust and relationships

        Trust and positive relationships between team members enable the team to collaborate without being derailed by personal ambitions or interpersonal misgivings. Establishing trust is an ongoing process. A good starting point is for team members to get to know each other as people, rather than just as coworkers. Each team member should also make an effort to behave in a trustworthy manner. Intrateam relationships can also be monitored through surveys.

C. Productive collaboration

Productive collaboration is the goal of a collaborative team. Once the team has established a base of norms and trust, the work the team does is what facilitates their effect on students. School leaders, as well as the team itself, should monitor the team's productivity using checklists or agendas or simply by looking at artifacts. If a team is collaborating productively, there will be clear evidence in the form of documents and other products.

5. **Describe one challenging aspect of the PLC process and how it can be mitigated.**

Answers will vary. One challenging aspect of the PLC process is that it takes time—often more than traditional systems. Groups often take longer to make decisions and, of course, school leaders need to find collaborative time in an already limited school schedule. Educators undertaking the PLC process can mitigate this issue first by simply being patient. They should not expect that implementing collaborative teams will be a fast process or a quick fix. People take time to adjust to any new system before they can reach peak effectiveness. Secondly, schools and teachers can make use of technology tools, such as shared documents, to allow teams to collaborate outside of meeting times.

Chapter 3 Comprehension Questions

1. **Why is a guaranteed and viable curriculum important?**

   A guaranteed and viable curriculum works to reduce variability in students' education. When the curriculum is viable, all the content can be taught in the instructional time available. Teachers do not have to make idiosyncratic decisions about what content to teach. Therefore, all teachers of a course or grade level deliver the same content to their students, guaranteeing the curriculum and creating consistency for all students.

2. **What are the four steps to creating a guaranteed and viable curriculum? Briefly describe each step.**

   The first step is to identify the essential content. This involves examining district or state standards and deciding which ones will be prioritized in the guaranteed and viable curriculum. The second step is to include cognitive and conative skills. The curriculum should not consist entirely of academic content standards; critical thinking and interpersonal skills should be taught as well. The third step is to identify learning goals or objectives. This means examining the prioritized standards and breaking them down into more focused, discrete parts. The fourth and final step is to construct proficiency scales. This process involves creating learning progressions for each objective.

3. **Why should standards be translated into learning goals or objectives?**

   Standards, as typically written, often include numerous subcomponents. One standard might encompass several individual elements that each require a separate proficiency scale. Alternatively, a standard might include some content that would be an appropriate target learning goal and some content that is simpler or foundational to the target. By breaking standards apart and rewriting their components as individual objectives, teachers can make the standards more useful and get a better sense of how much content there really is.

4. **Explain each level of a proficiency scale.**

   Score 3.0 represents the target learning goal. A student who has reached this level is proficient with the content. Score 4.0 represents a more complex learning goal that goes beyond what was directly taught in class. Score 2.0 is the simpler learning goal—content that must be mastered before a student can reach proficiency. Score 1.0 indicates that, with prompting from the teacher, a student can demonstrate partial knowledge of levels 2.0 and 3.0. Score 0.0 indicates no knowledge, even with help. The half-point scores between the levels indicate success at the level below and partial success at the level above. For example, a score 2.5 indicates complete knowledge of the score 2.0 content and partial knowledge of the score 3.0 content.

Chapter 4 Comprehension Questions

1. **Why are proficiency scales a useful basis from which to create assessments?**

   Proficiency scales very clearly define various levels of knowledge in relation to a learning goal. Assessments are intended to determine a student's level of knowledge. The information in a proficiency scale can be used to create an assessment whose items very clearly match up with and indicate specific levels of proficiency.

2. **When creating an assessment blueprint, how many and what types of items are generally appropriate for each level of the proficiency scale?**

   Assessment of score 2.0 content usually involves numerous short, forced-choice items, such as multiple-choice questions. Typically, five or more questions are needed to assess this level. Items that assess score 3.0 content require students to access multiple pieces of content and often take the form of short written responses. An assessment usually includes two or more items at this level. Score 4.0 assessment items also require that students synthesize numerous aspects of the content as well as make inferences or applications that go beyond what was taught in class. This level is often assessed by an extended essay question.

3. **Why should collaborative teams administer common assessments to their students and discuss the results as a group?**

   When teachers use common assessments, they can compare the results from various classes to identify common trends and areas of difference. For example, they might find that many students in multiple classes answered a particular item incorrectly. This might lead to a discussion about reteaching the content or revising the assessment item. The team might also find that some classes did well on an item or section that another class struggled with. In this case, teachers can share instructional strategies that might help the latter class achieve proficiency in that area. Finally, common assessment results can be used to identify students for intervention or extension, which can be done as a team.

4. **Identify and describe the three broad types of assessment that can be used to gauge student learning.**

   The three broad types of assessment are obtrusive, unobtrusive, and student-generated. Obtrusive assessments, such as pen-and-paper tests or oral presentations, require stopping instruction while students complete them. Unobtrusive assessments occur when the teacher observes a student demonstrating learning during the course of instruction and records an assessment score. Student-generated assessments are initiated by the student rather than the teacher; a student identifies a way that he or she can demonstrate a level of proficiency and takes responsibility for completing that task.

Chapter 5 Comprehension Questions

1. **What are the two types of planning in which collaborative teams should engage?**

   The first type of planning is planning for high-quality initial instruction. This means preparing lessons and units in advance so that students have the best possible opportunity to learn the content during the first round of instruction. The second type is planning after common assessments. During this stage, teachers determine how they will use information from the assessment to make sure that students get the intervention or extension they need.

2. **What are the three broad categories of lessons? How do these categories link content to instruction?**

   The three categories of lessons are (1) direct instruction lessons, (2) practicing and deepening lessons, and (3) knowledge application lessons. In the first type, the teacher presents (typically new) content directly to students. In the second type, the teacher helps students increase their depth of knowledge or their fluency with skills and processes. In the third type, the teacher guides students through cognitively complex tasks that require students to apply what they've learned in new ways. These categories of lessons link content to instruction by helping teachers examine the nature of specific content and which instructional strategies will be most effective for presenting it.

3. **Describe one way that a collaborative team can respond to student needs identified based on assessment results.**

   A collaborative team can respond to student needs based on assessment results by grouping students according to their current levels of proficiency. Students who are not yet proficient may require continued instruction or intervention, while students who have demonstrated proficiency can engage in extension activities. A collaborative team can use members' combined resources to temporarily regroup all their students into leveled groups and assign teachers to each one.

4. **Explain the process of lesson study.**

   Lesson study is an iterative process by which a team of teachers collaboratively creates and develops a lesson. First, the team does the initial planning of the lesson based on a specific learning goal. Then, one teacher teaches the lesson while the others observe. After the observation, the teachers discuss the lesson and how students responded to it. Based on this discussion, the team makes changes to the lesson plan. Another teacher implements this new version of the lesson, and the process continues.

5. **How do the tiers of RTI relate to the levels of a proficiency scale?**

   Tier 1 of RTI involves high-quality initial instruction at levels 2.0 and 3.0 of a proficiency scale. Students who still score below proficient on the content within the scale after general Tier 1 instruction move to Tier 2 of RTI: supplemental instruction. Tier 3 of RTI relates to more severe needs outside the content of the proficiency scale.

Chapter 6 Comprehension Questions

1. **Why are collaborative teams an appropriate and effective forum for teacher development?**

The ultimate goal of a collaborative team is to improve student learning. As teacher effectiveness is one of the biggest influences on how much students learn, increasing instructional ability is an extremely worthwhile endeavor for a collaborative team. When teachers work together to develop professionally, they can learn from each other. In this situation, teamwork is extremely effective because different teachers have various areas of expertise and can act as models as well as give constructive feedback to others. Collaborative teams are also a good vehicle for professional development because activities around improvement can be embedded throughout the school year instead of occurring only as occasional workshops.

2. **Describe the process of instructional rounds. What purposes can this process serve?**

During instructional rounds, a small group of teachers observes a part of a lesson that another teacher is presenting. They silently take notes and then leave to debrief their observations. Instructional rounds can be used to observe a model of the effective use of a strategy, in which case the group would discuss the positive things they saw and want to try. Another use of instructional rounds is as a method of peer feedback, in which case the group would discuss both positive notes and opportunities for improvement. In either case, the products of the group's discussion should be shared with the observed teacher.

3. **How can a collaborative team implement reflective practice?**

To engage in reflective practice as a team, members can either select a single common growth goal or individual growth goals. A growth goal is typically a specific strategy or element of teaching with which one wants to become more fluent. Whether a team has chosen individual goals or a group goal, the focused practice phase of reflective practice is undertaken by each teacher individually. Then, the collaborative team gives feedback to each member by observing them either in person or on video.

4. **What is the role of student feedback in a PLC? How can teachers obtain student feedback?**

Students and their learning are the focus of the PLC process; therefore, educators in a PLC should seek student input so they can maximize their positive effects on students. The simplest way to obtain student feedback is through the use of surveys.

5. **What is action research? What are its benefits?**

Action research is when teachers evaluate instructional strategies by trying them out and measuring their effects on students. The teacher chooses an instructional strategy and two classes of students—one class is the experimental group and receives instruction *with* the chosen strategy, while the other class is the comparison group that receives instruction *without* the strategy. Both classes receive the same pretest and posttest, and the teacher compares the amount of knowledge growth per class. Action research has the benefit of being a quantitative measure of the effectiveness of an instructional strategy. Rather than basing one's use of strategies on a general perception that they seem to be working, one can use action research to truly test their efficacy.

Chapter 7 Comprehension Questions

1. **Describe the importance of effective leadership to the PLC process.**

   School leaders have the capacity to implement the PLC process across the whole school, which is a requirement for a truly effective PLC. School leaders do have a measurable, though indirect effect on student learning, so it is important that they are just as committed to the PLC process as classroom teachers.

2. **What is second-order change?**

   Second-order change is change that requires substantial shifts in basic thinking, philosophies, and approaches to doing business.

3. **How does leadership for second-order change differ from leadership for more basic changes?**

   Leadership for second-order change requires focusing on specific elements of effective leadership, such as ideals and beliefs, monitoring and evaluating, and being the driving force behind the change. Because second-order change is so significant and innovative, leaders must be continually involved at a much deeper level than they might be with first-order change.

4. **What does it mean to "distribute leadership" or "flatten an organization"? Why is this important in a PLC?**

   Flattening an organization or distributing leadership means that leadership responsibilities are held by a wider group of people. Rather than a small group of school administrators making decisions with teachers following, leaders provide vision or direction, and collaborative teams are given autonomy within those bounds. Distributing leadership also means involving stakeholders in decision-making processes. For example, a school's leadership team might be expanded to include teachers, or leaders might hold open meetings in which teachers can participate.

APPENDIX B

Resources for Collaborative Teams

This appendix contains resources that collaborative teams can use to establish group norms, collaborate productively, and interact responsibly.

Group Norms

As discussed in chapter 2 (page 17), establishing group norms is an important early step for collaborative teams. It is also essential that teams continue to abide by and monitor these norms as time goes on. To facilitate the maintenance of norms, a team might create a chart like the example in figure 2.1 (page 25). The first column lists each of the team's norms. The second and third columns make the norms more concrete by describing examples and nonexamples (respectively) of adherence to the norm. The last column, titled Rating, allows the chart to be used as a survey. The team could periodically have its members rate the group's performance on each norm as a way to monitor collaborative behavior. Collaborative teams can use the reproducible chart on the next page to create and track their own norms.

Norm Chart

Norm	Example	Nonexample	Rating

Agendas

To make sure they stay on track with their work, teams can use detailed agendas. First, a checklist of long-term projects can help provide an overview of important tasks. Figure A.1 depicts an example of this type of long-term agenda. Each row includes the task, details about what needs to be done to complete it, and a deadline. In this example, the team has set deadlines for beginning-of-the-year tasks and tasks to start preparing for second term. The reproducible version (page 129) allows collaborative teams to set their own long-term schedule.

Task	Specific Details	Deadline
Review of Norms	Work begins on Monday, August 24, at the staff meeting. It will be continued (if required) at collaborative team meetings that week.	Please return team norms to Nathan or Ingrid by Friday, August 29.
Review of Prioritized Standards	Review prioritized standards to ensure that there are an appropriate number and they meet all of the essential learning criteria. This is to be done during the collaborative team meeting after school on Wednesday, September 3.	The review will be completed during this meeting.
Review of Schedule	Review the class schedule and discuss the options available to their team for the provision of common weekly intervention times.	Please turn in schedule draft options to Nathan or Ingrid by Friday, September 12.
Creation of SMART Goal Around State Summative Assessment Data	Review last year's state summative assessment data. As a team, set a SMART goal for student achievement for this year.	Please turn in SMART goals to Nathan or Ingrid by Friday, September 19.
Creation of Term Two Pacing Guide	Draft a pacing guide for the prioritized standards to be covered during term two.	Please turn in the first draft of pacing guide to Nathan or Ingrid by Friday, October 3.

Figure A.1: Sample long-term agenda.

To plan for and stay on track during individual meetings, teams can use more detailed agendas with tasks, time limits, and results. Figure A.2 (page 128) shows an example agenda of this type. The team that created this agenda has chosen to assign specific meeting roles, such as timekeeper—the person who makes sure that the group sticks to the schedule defined by the Time Allocated column. This team also chooses a focus norm for each meeting. The agenda itself includes a list of objectives for the meeting, the time allocated for each one, and the results of the discussion. The list of objectives and specific questions below each one are planned before the meeting, as is the time limit schedule. During the meeting, the team records decisions and action items that result from the discussion in the Results column. Collaborative teams can use the reproducible agenda (page 130) to plan individual meetings.

Team Meeting: Monday, November 17		
Timekeeper: Lenis Norm Monitor: Natalie Minute Taker: Steph		
Focus Norm: Participation	We will show our commitment to this norm by: • Explicitly asking for input if necessary • Encouraging sharing • Listening to new ideas and questions without judgment • Offering input	
Time Allocated	**Task**	**Results**
10 minutes	Numeracy: Sorting & Patterns • What do the data show? • What does that mean? • What are the next steps?	Continue to work with all students to sort objects in different ways. Whole-class focus lessons will be based around tuning students into sorting by attributes other than color.
10 minutes	Writing: Writing Moderation • What topic will we write about? • What are we looking for? • How will we assess it?	Nature walk: Students will use magnifying glasses to investigate things they see in nature. Before the walk, alert students that there will be a writing component at the end. After the walk, brainstorm ideas on the board with the class and model a writing piece before asking students to write independently.
15 minutes	Common Assessment Results: Magnetism • What trends do we see? • How should we plan lessons for students who haven't reached proficiency? • Does the assessment need to be modified?	All students can explain how distance affects the interaction of magnets, but some haven't been able to apply attraction and repulsion to simple engineering problems. During independent work time, we will pull these students into small-group instruction and use hands-on activities and guiding questions to increase their understanding of the practical uses of magnets. The assessment seems sound; there were no uneven or aberrant response patterns.
5 minutes	Reflection on Focus Norm • Did we see the norm being followed? • What did it look and sound like? • Do we need to improve on this norm?	Everyone on the team participates during discussion, but not always on every topic. We can improve by asking team members if they have anything to add before moving on to the next topic.

Figure A.2: Sample meeting agenda.

Long-Term Agenda

Task	Specific Details	Deadline

Meeting Agenda

Meeting Agenda for: _____

Meeting Date: _____ Time: _____ Place: _____

Facilitator: _____

Participants: _____

Meeting Tasks

Time Limit	Objective	Results

Discussion Guidelines

Communicating responsibly is essential in collaborative teams, especially during difficult conversations. Honest and forthright discussion is critical to success: "When teams avoid conflict, they are playing nice at the expense of real progress" (Graham & Ferriter, 2010, p. 108). Teams should have norms that address conversation but may be further aided by examples and guidelines that help members communicate assertively without becoming aggressive. Team members can distribute or display the following reproducibles to encourage effective and conscientious communication.

Sentence Stems for Communicating Responsibly

When engaging in a discussion, participants must clearly convey their ideas while remaining respectful of others. The following sentence stems provide guidance for various conversational goals, specifically: clarifying a point, connecting a statement to other points, agreeing and disagreeing with other participants, changing the subject, and taking responsibility for one's own communication.

Clarifying	Connecting
How is this relevant to your point? Can you explain what you mean? So what you're saying is _____.	I want to say more about what _____ said about _____. I'd like to add _____. I noticed that _____. What _____ said reminded me of _____.

Agreeing	Disagreeing
I agree with _____ because _____. I think _____ made a great point about _____. Yes, and furthermore, _____. Although we still disagree on the claim overall, it seems to me that we *can* agree on _____.	I disagree with _____ because _____. Couldn't it also be that _____? I see why _____ might say that, but _____. While I think _____ had a point that _____, I disagree with the part where he/she said _____. It seems to me that _____ committed an error in reasoning when he/she said _____.

Changing the Subject	Taking Responsibility
It seems to me that we're spending a lot of time discussing _____, when maybe we should be discussing _____. I'd like to change the subject to _____. Something I think the other side has not addressed is _____.	I must have miscommunicated my point earlier; I apologize. What I intended to say was _____. Earlier, I neglected to point out _____. I'm sorry, I misunderstood you. I thought you meant _____. You're right. Those words were hurtful and uncalled for. I shouldn't have said that.

Source: Rogers, K., & Simms, J. A. (2015). Teaching argumentation: Activities and games for the classroom. *Bloomington, IN: Marzano Research, pp. 44–45.*

Conversational Skills

These conversational protocols (Hord & Sommers, 2008) provide simple guidelines for respectful and productive discussions.

- **Listen:** Focus on what is being said instead of waiting for your turn to speak.

- **Set aside judgment:** Remain open to various perspectives and new ideas.

- **Ask questions:** Seek clarity before making a decision about what has been said.

- **Make observations:** State your perspective or restate another person's perspective without passing judgment.

- **Stay open:** Let the discussion run its course; do not force judgments or decisions too soon.

- **Clarify goals:** Restate and ask questions to clarify the goal of the conversation; shift focus to what we do want, rather than what we don't want.

Source: Hord, S. M., & Sommers, W. A. (2008). Leading professional learning communities: Voices from research and practice. *Thousand Oaks, CA: Corwin Press.*

Reconciling Opposing Ideas

In collaborative teams, decision making is a regular and frequent activity. Often, various members of the group will propose different ideas or options. When two or more options seem feasible and beneficial, it can be difficult to come to a final decision. If the decision-making process stalls, teams can use strategies such as perspective taking and synthesis to move forward.

Perspective Taking

When team members are having a hard time coming to a consensus, they can try an exercise in perspective analysis (Johnson & Johnson, 2007; Marzano, 1992; Marzano & Heflebower, 2012). First, they should identify and argue for their own view, using reasoning and evidence and seeking to explain the perspective as fully as possible. Then, the parties trade perspectives and each person defends the other's view. Parties should make an effort to explain and support the opposing view as well and completely as they did their own. This helps people understand why others hold certain opinions and can make compromise more feasible. Finally, team members should make this new understanding explicit by summarizing what they have learned or how their perspective has changed as a result.

Synthesis

When a consensus or course of action is required, sometimes it is best to synthesize two seemingly opposing ideas (Johnson & Johnson, 2007). The first requirement for this process is for all parties to become as objective as possible and stop advocating for their personal positions. Then the group must dispassionately analyze the evidence or parts of each option based on objective quality. Using these best aspects from each side, the group should synthesize a new, combinatorial option. This process helps the group "arrive at the best possible position on the issue and . . . find a position that all group members can agree and commit themselves to" (Johnson & Johnson, 2007, chapter 7, p. 6).

Sources:

Johnson, D. W., & Johnson, R. T. (2007). Creative controversy: Intellectual challenge in the classroom (4th ed.). *Edina, MN: Interaction Book.*

Marzano, R. J. (1992). A different kind of classroom: Teaching with dimensions of learning. *Alexandria, VA: Association for Supervision and Curriculum Development.*

Marzano, R. J., & Heflebower, T. (2012). Teaching and assessing 21st century skills. *Bloomington, IN: Marzano Research.*

Confronting Difficult Topics

In long-term collaborative work, difficult topics and situations will almost inevitably arise. Difficult situations could emerge from the group's work itself, such as one person strongly objecting to a decision made by the group, but could also be more personal, such as a member feeling that he or she is treated unfairly by the rest of the group. To preserve the group's ability to work productively together, these kinds of issues must be dealt with directly, rather than allowed to fester. The following sections describe ways to proactively address difficult issues.

General Guidelines for Confrontation

These seven guidelines for confrontation (adapted from Maxwell, 1995) outline the basic steps for addressing a challenging situation.

1. Conduct the discussion as soon as possible.

2. Focus on the behavior or action, not the person.

3. Be specific.

4. Give the person an opportunity to respond, and grant him or her the benefit of the doubt.

5. Avoid sarcasm and absolutes such as *always* and *never*.

6. Attempt to develop a mutual plan to address the problem.

7. Affirm the person.

Remaining Civil

Remaining polite and civil during difficult discussions is essential for keeping the discussion productive, reaching a solution, and maintaining positive relationships between participants. The following four aspects of civil interaction (Patterson, Grenny, McMillan, & Switzler, 2002) can keep debates from becoming too heated, emotional, or hurtful.

1. **Identify your motive:** Be honest with yourself and others about the issue at hand. When confrontations break out unexpectedly, they often seem to be about a surface issue but are really about a different underlying problem. To start a productive conversation, explicitly identify the problem you want to discuss.

2. **Make it safe:** Be proactive to prevent defensiveness and hurt feelings. First, express appreciation and respect for other people in the discussion. Second, establish shared purpose—often, two people with differing opinions have the same end goal in mind. Third, use structured responses to express a balance of positive and negative statements; for example, "I *don't* want you to feel as though I'm attacking or discrediting your ideas— you have a lot of really great ones—but I *do* want you to know that I feel like my ideas are automatically rejected because I'm the newest member of the team."

3. **Master your own emotions:** Make an effort to prevent emotional reactions. State facts about what happened and then state how those events made you feel instead of blaming another person or speculating about someone else's opinions or motivations.

page 1 of 2

4. **Work to understand others' perspectives:** Listen actively to opposing viewpoints. Assume that the other person has good reasons and good intentions behind what he or she says and does. Try to reach mutual understanding rather than forcing the other person to see things your way.

Conflict Management Questions

When discussing a controversial issue requires that a decision be made, it can be helpful to take a structured approach. The following six conflict management questions (Chadwick, 1995) frame the issue and lead the group toward the best possible outcome.

Allow everyone in the group to express their feelings and opinions in response to each question.

1. What are the issues surrounding this topic and how do you feel about it?

2. What is the worst possible outcome if we don't address this problem? What is the worst possible outcome if we do address this problem?

3. What is the best possible outcome if we don't address this problem? What is the best possible outcome if we do address this problem?

4. What beliefs and values are necessary for us to foster the best possible outcome?

5. What strategies and actions are you willing to take in order to foster the best possible outcomes?

6. What will be the evidence that we are fostering our best possible outcome?

Negotiation

If two sides are at odds with each other and need to reach consensus, they can negotiate. The following six negotiation steps (Johnson & Johnson, 2005) involve sharing information before inventing new options (which might include elements from both sides) and coming to a mutually acceptable agreement.

1. Describe what you want.

2. Describe your feelings.

3. Exchange reasons for positions.

4. Understand the other person's perspective.

5. Invent options.

6. Reach an agreement.

Sources:

Chadwick, B. (1995). Conflict to consensus workshop. *Minneapolis, MN: Minneapolis Public Schools.*

Johnson, D. W., & Johnson, R. T. (2005). Teaching students to be peacemakers (4th ed.). *Edina, MN: Interaction Book.*

Maxwell, J. (1995). Developing the leaders around you: How to help others reach their full potential. *Nashville, TN: Nelson.*

Patterson, K., Grenny, J., McMillan, R., & Switzler, A. (2002). Crucial conversations: Tools for talking when stakes are high. *New York: McGraw-Hill Education.*

Collaborative Team Rating Scales

Collaborative teams should periodically conduct formal audits of their collaboration and productivity. This scale, modeled after a proficiency scale, is intended to help collaborative teams measure their progress with regard to the functionality of the team. Teams can assess what level of the scale they have reached by comparing their work to the descriptions and sample indicators in figure A.3. Teams or schools can also use the blank reproducible (page 138) to create a customized autonomy scale and record evidence of their work at each level.

Score	Description	Indicators
Score 4.0	Operational Autonomy • Collective ownership of student achievement is evident in practice and products. • Productive culture of collaboration is evident in practice and products. • SMART goals are clearly defined and progress toward goals is monitored. • The norms guide all practice and are evaluated for effectiveness by the team.	Critical areas such as curriculum, instruction, assessment, and teacher development are the focus of meetings and agenda items. Common assessment data are a key element of team decision making. SMART goal progress monitoring is in place. Periodically, the team reviews the norms to ensure they are being followed.
Score 3.0	Developing Autonomy • Collective ownership of student achievement is emerging in some practices and products. • Collaborative culture is emerging but not constant in practices and products. • SMART goals are clearly defined. • The norms are established and members hold themselves and each other accountable to the norms.	Critical areas such as curriculum, instruction, assessment, and teacher development are sometimes the focus of meetings and agenda items. Collaboration is taking place on most issues within the scope of the collaborative team. SMART goals are appropriate and clearly defined.
Score 2.0	Partial Autonomy • Individual ownership of student achievement is the predominant practice among team members. • Collaboration is occurring on specific issues. • SMART goals are defined but may need revision. • The norms are established and individuals hold themselves accountable to the norms.	Teachers operate with a more individual focus on their practice and their specific students. Some aspects of team collaboration are beginning to occur.
Score 1.0	No Autonomy • Norms have not been established. • SMART goals have not been established. • Collaboration is not evident.	Teachers actively avoid collaboration in favor of working alone.

Figure A.3: Collaborative team autonomy scale.

Autonomy Scale

Score	Description	Indicators
Score 4.0	Operational Autonomy	
Score 3.0	Developing Autonomy	
Score 2.0	Partial Autonomy	
Score 1.0	No Autonomy	

APPENDIX C

The New Taxonomy

This appendix also appeared in **Proficiency Scales for the New Science Standards: A Framework for Science Instruction and Assessment** *(Marzano & Yanoski, 2016).*

The taxonomy presented here is part of a more comprehensive framework titled *The New Taxonomy of Educational Objectives* (Marzano & Kendall, 2007; see also Marzano & Kendall, 2008). Robert J. Marzano (2009) previously described the relationship between this taxonomy and designing and teaching learning goals and objectives in *Designing & Teaching Learning Goals & Objectives.*

The taxonomy includes four levels.

- Level 4 (Knowledge Utilization)
- Level 3 (Analysis)
- Level 2 (Comprehension)
- Level 1 (Retrieval)

To understand the taxonomy as it applies to academic content, it is necessary to address two types of knowledge: (1) declarative knowledge and (2) procedural knowledge. Declarative knowledge is informational content that can be conceptualized as a hierarchy in its own right. At the bottom of the declarative knowledge hierarchy is vocabulary—terms and phrases about which an individual has an accurate but not necessarily deep understanding. Facts reside a level above vocabulary terms and phrases. The highest level of the declarative knowledge hierarchy consists of generalizations, principles, and concepts.

Procedural knowledge includes mental procedures and psychomotor procedures. Both mental procedures and psychomotor procedures exist in a hierarchy as well. The lowest level of the mental procedures hierarchy contains single rules like those a writer might use when determining proper punctuation for an essay. The level immediately above single rules contains algorithms and tactics. A person will have an algorithm for multiplying two-digit numbers and a tactic (also known as a strategy) for how to read a bar graph. Macroprocesses reside at the highest level of the mental procedure hierarchy and can be thought of as arrays of single rules, algorithms, and tactics organized into an interacting set. For example, writing might best be described as a macroprocess. Psychomotor procedures also exist in a hierarchy. Foundational procedures like static strength, manual dexterity, and arm-hand steadiness are situated at the bottom of the hierarchy. A level up from foundational procedures are simple combination procedures like shooting a free throw in basketball. The highest psychomotor level involves complex combination procedures like guarding an opponent in basketball.

Level 1 (Retrieval)

The process of retrieval varies depending on the type of knowledge involved and the degree of processing required. There are three types of retrieval: (1) recognizing, (2) recalling, and (3) executing. The first two types apply to both declarative and procedural knowledge, while the third type applies only to procedural knowledge.

Recognizing Goals

Recognizing determines whether information is accurate or inaccurate. For example, a goal that requires students to select a synonym for a word from a word list relies on recognition. The teacher provides a synonym to the student, and the student must recognize its alternative. Examples of recognizing goals for the various types of knowledge include the following.

Declarative Knowledge: Students will be able to identify the sequence of critical events leading up to the outbreak of World War II in Europe.

Mental Procedures: Students will be able to identify a pie chart among a list of charts as appropriate for representing proportional data.

Psychomotor Procedures: Students will be able to acknowledge that cross-checking is an important defensive strategy in ice hockey.

Recalling Goals

Recalling requires students to produce information from permanent memory. Thus, a goal requiring students to produce a synonym for a specific term employs recall. This is more difficult than simply recognizing the correct example from a provided list. That is, recalling involves producing accurate information as opposed to simply recognizing it. Examples of recalling goals for the various types of knowledge include the following.

Declarative Knowledge: Students will be able to provide everyday examples that demonstrate the law of unbalanced forces.

Mental Procedures: Students will be able to recall that heart and breathing rates are components of a fitness assessment.

Psychomotor Procedures: Students will be able to recall that left hand positioning and strength of grip are crucial aspects of playing the guitar.

Executing Goals

Executing refers only to procedural knowledge and involves actually carrying out a mental or psychomotor procedure, as opposed to simply recognizing or recalling information about it. To illustrate, consider the mental procedure of multicolumn subtraction. A teacher could write a recognizing goal for this procedure that requires students to identify accurate statements about multicolumn subtraction. The teacher could write a recalling goal that requires students to describe how to perform multicolumn subtraction. Neither goal actually asks a student to perform the process of multicolumn subtraction, however. This is the role of execution—asking a student to demonstrate a skill, strategy, or process.

There is a great deal of misunderstanding regarding executing goals, particularly as they relate to complex mental and psychomotor procedures. Although it is true that executing is at the lowest level of the taxonomy (because it is a form of retrieval), executing can be a difficult task for students, particularly when a complex mental or psychomotor procedure is involved. Consider the mental procedure of writing a persuasive essay. The actual execution of this process is a complex feat indeed, requiring the management of many interacting components. This is why writing is referred to as a macroprocess. The same can be said for the psychomotor procedure of playing basketball.

How, then, does one differentiate the level of difficulty for a complex procedure like writing? One way is to break the procedure into smaller component parts. For example, students less skilled at writing persuasive essays might focus on stating a clear claim and writing a few sentences to support the claim. Goals for students more skilled at constructing persuasive essays would incorporate additional components of the overall complex procedure into the process. For example, the more advanced students might also specify that each piece of evidence should be backed up with information supporting its validity.

Like writing a persuasive essay, playing basketball includes a variety of embedded procedures. For less skilled students, a goal might focus only on dribbling. A goal for more skilled students might include dribbling while running down the court and passing the ball to other players. Again, as the level of difficulty increases, the procedure involves more component procedures acting in tandem.

Examples of executing goals for mental and psychomotor procedures include the following.

Mental Procedures: Students will be able to monitor and interpret heart rate and breathing rate.

Psychomotor Procedures: Students will be able to type at a reasonable speed using correct hand positioning.

Level 2 (Comprehension)

Comprehension processes require students to demonstrate an understanding of the overall structure of knowledge—the critical versus noncritical aspects of the knowledge. There are two related types of comprehension processes: (1) integrating and (2) symbolizing.

Integrating Goals

Integrating involves distilling knowledge down to its key characteristics and organizing the characteristics into a parsimonious, generalized form. Thus, integrating goals require students to describe the critical—as opposed to noncritical—information regarding content. Examples of integrating goals for the various types of knowledge include the following.

Declarative Knowledge: Students will be able to provide a description showing how the tilt and revolution of the Earth around the sun affect the seasons.

Mental Procedures: Students will be able to describe the key steps involved in selecting a random sample.

Psychomotor Procedures: Students will be able to explain the nuances of applying colors and forms in landscape painting when using a specific set of brush strokes.

Symbolizing Goals

Symbolizing requires students to translate their understanding into a graphic representation. In other words, symbolizing goals require students to translate what they have produced from an integrating goal into a nonlinguistic form. Consequently, symbolizing goals are frequently used in tandem with integrating goals. Examples of symbolizing goals for the various types of knowledge include the following.

Declarative Knowledge: Students will be able to graphically depict the relationship between supply and demand.

Mental Procedures: Students will be able to represent the flow of an information search on the Internet using text features and hierarchic structures in web-based information text.

Psychomotor Procedures: Students will be able to illustrate an S-turn, indicating the position of a skier's torso and skis relative to the fall line as well as the changing pressure on the uphill and downhill skis throughout the turn.

Level 3 (Analysis)

Analysis processes require students to go beyond what was actually taught in class to make inferences that create new awareness. There are five types of analysis processes: (1) matching, (2) classifying, (3) analyzing errors, (4) generalizing, and (5) specifying.

Matching Goals

Matching involves identifying similarities and differences. Examples of matching goals for the various types of knowledge include the following.

Declarative Knowledge: Students will be able to describe the similarities and differences between the terms *power* and *authority*.

Mental Procedures: Students will be able to describe what is similar and different about the processes of determining the validity of a primary source and a secondary source.

Psychomotor Procedures: Students will be able to describe how using a graphite pencil is similar to and different from using a charcoal pencil when sketching a face.

Classifying Goals

Classifying goes beyond organizing items into groups or categories (such an activity is better thought of as matching). Instead, classifying involves identifying the superordinate category into which knowledge belongs, as well as any subordinate categories. To illustrate, a goal that requires students to organize the fifty states into three categories based on voting tendencies in presidential elections (Democratic, Republican, or Independent) is considered a classifying task, because it requires students to identify the superordinate category to which each state belongs. Conversely, a learning goal that asks students to organize the fifty states into categories of their own choosing would be considered a matching goal, because it requires students to organize states by similarities and differences of their own design. Examples of classifying goals for the various types of knowledge include the following.

Declarative Knowledge: Students will be able to classify food by its relative amount of protein, fat, and vitamins.

Mental Procedures: Students will be able to identify gestures as a type of nonverbal communication.

Psychomotor Procedures: Students will be able to classify a set of strategies as common to net games as opposed to invasion games.

Analyzing Errors Goals

Analyzing errors requires students to identify factual or logical errors in declarative knowledge or processing errors in the execution of procedural knowledge. Examples of analyzing errors goals for the various types of knowledge include the following.

Declarative Knowledge: Students will be able to identify what is plausible and implausible about the characters in a given story.

Mental Procedures: Students will be able to identify flaws in graph presentation based on skill at interpreting the x and y axes.

Psychomotor Procedures: Students will be able to identify technical errors in technique for a chosen instrument.

Generalizing Goals

Generalizing requires students to infer new abstractions or principles from known or stated information. Generalizing goals involve inductive thinking, in that students must create broad statements based on specific pieces of information. Examples of generalizing goals for the various types of knowledge include the following.

Declarative Knowledge: Students will be able to make and defend generalizations about the influence of a source of information on the validity of the information presented.

Mental Procedures: Students will be able to construct and defend generalizations about the use of specific refusal skills used in social situations.

Psychomotor Procedures: Students will be able to generalize about the relationship between movement forms in sports and movement forms of machines mimicking those sports.

Specifying Goals

Specifying requires students to make and defend predictions about what might happen in a given situation. The process of specifying is deductive in nature, as it requires students to reason from a rule or principle to make and defend a prediction. Examples of specifying goals for the various types of knowledge include the following.

> **Declarative Knowledge:** Students will be able to identify circumstances that indicate the occurrence of processes that quickly or slowly change the Earth.

> **Mental Procedures:** Students will be able to make and defend inferences about measurement results based on an understanding of the relationship between perimeter and area.

> **Psychomotor Procedures:** Students will be able to make and defend inferences about the likely strategy of a tennis opponent when presented with consistent behaviors of the opponent.

Level 4 (Knowledge Utilization)

Knowledge utilization processes require students to apply or use knowledge in specific situations. There are four types of knowledge utilization processes: (1) decision making, (2) problem solving, (3) experimenting, and (4) investigating.

Decision-Making Goals

Decision making requires students to select among choices that initially appear equal. Examples of decision-making goals for the various types of knowledge include the following.

> **Declarative Knowledge:** Students will be able to decide on the props and scenery for a stage setting of Denmark in the year 2050 based on an understanding of effective stage design.

> **Mental Procedures:** Students will be able to decide, based on an understanding of specific learning strategies, the best way to learn new, personally chosen content.

> **Psychomotor Procedures:** Students will be able to decide, based on an understanding of painting techniques, how to best create a specific visual effect.

Problem-Solving Goals

Problem solving requires students to accomplish a goal for which obstacles or limiting conditions exist. Problem solving and decision making are closely related in that decision making frequently serves as a sub-component in the process of problem solving. However, whereas decision making does not involve obstacles to a goal, problem solving does. Examples of problem-solving goals for the various types of knowledge include the following.

> **Declarative Knowledge:** Students will be able to propose a solution for the adoption of a specific alternative energy source based on an understanding of the obstacles and trade-offs associated with its use.

Mental Procedures: Students will be able to identify how best to solve a problem of negative social influence through an understanding of the best use of refusal skills.

Psychomotor Procedures: Students will be able to solve a specific fingering problem for the guitar by revising fingering notation to consider personal skills and limitations.

Experimenting Goals

Experimenting requires students to generate and test hypotheses about a specific physical or psychological phenomenon. Experimenting requires that the data are newly collected by students. That is, students must use data that they have generated themselves. Examples of experimenting goals for the various types of knowledge include the following.

Declarative Knowledge: Students will be able to generate and test a hypothesis that demonstrates an understanding of the possible impact of recent technology on society.

Mental Procedures: Students will be able to generate a hypothesis regarding which map projection will provide more and less accurate data about the distance between two places and test that hypothesis through measurement.

Psychomotor Procedures: Students will be able to generate and test a hypothesis about the ease or difficulty of using specific left-hand positions when playing a specific chord progression on the guitar.

Investigating Goals

Investigating requires students to examine a past, present, or future situation. Investigating is similar to experimenting in that it involves the gathering and testing of data. However, the data used in investigation are not gathered by direct observation on the part of the student (as they are in experimentation). Instead, the data used in investigation are assertions and opinions made by others. Investigating may be likened more to investigative reporting, whereas experimenting may be likened more to pure scientific inquiry. Examples of investigating goals for the various types of knowledge include the following.

Declarative Knowledge: Students will be able to investigate how acquiring daily food placed great demands on families in the 1800s.

Mental Procedures: Students will be able to investigate how specific methods of measuring weight have changed over time.

Psychomotor Procedures: Students will be able to investigate how and why changes in sports equipment can impact skills required for a specific sport.

A Model of Effective Instruction

Feedback

Providing and Communicating Clear Learning Goals

Providing Scales and Rubrics	The teacher provides a clearly stated learning goal accompanied by a scale or rubric that describes levels of performance relative to the learning goal.
Tracking Student Progress	The teacher facilitates tracking of student progress on one or more learning goals using a formative approach to assessment.
Celebrating Success	The teacher provides students with recognition of their current status and their knowledge gain relative to the learning goal.

Assessment

Informal Assessments of the Whole Class	The teacher uses informal assessments of the whole class to determine student proficiency with specific content.
Formal Assessments of Individual Students	The teacher uses formal assessments of individual students to determine student proficiency with specific content.

Content

Direct Instruction Lessons

Chunking Content	Based on student needs, the teacher breaks the content into small chunks (that is, digestible bites) of information that can be easily processed by students.

Processing Content	During breaks in the presentation of content, the teacher engages students in actively processing new information.
Recording and Representing Content	The teacher engages students in activities that help them record their understanding of new content in linguistic ways and/or represent the content in nonlinguistic ways.

Practicing and Deepening Lessons

Structured Practice Sessions	When the content involves a skill, strategy, or process, the teacher engages students in practice activities that help them develop fluency.
Examining Similarities and Differences	When the content is informational, the teacher helps students deepen their knowledge by examining similarities and differences.
Examining Errors in Reasoning	When content is informational, the teacher helps students deepen their knowledge by examining their own reasoning or the logic of the information as presented to them.

Knowledge Application Lessons

Engaging Students in Cognitively Complex Tasks	The teacher engages students in complex tasks (for example, decision-making, problem-solving, experimental-inquiry, and investigation tasks) that require them to generate and test hypotheses.
Providing Resources and Guidance	The teacher acts as resource provider and guide as students engage in cognitively complex tasks.
Generating and Defending Claims	The teacher helps students create claims, or "new ideas," and defend them logically.

Strategies That Appear in All Types of Lessons

Previewing	The teacher engages students in activities that help them link what they already know to the new content and facilitates these linkages.
Highlighting Critical Information	The teacher identifies a lesson or part of a lesson as involving important information to which students should pay particular attention.
Reviewing Content	The teacher engages students in a brief review of content that highlights the critical information.
Revising Knowledge	The teacher engages students in revision of knowledge about content addressed in previous lessons.
Reflecting on Learning	The teacher engages students in activities that help them reflect on their learning and the learning process.
Purposeful Homework	When appropriate (as opposed to routinely), the teacher designs homework to deepen students' knowledge of informational content or practice a skill, strategy, or process.

| Elaborating on Information | The teacher asks questions or engages students in activities that require elaborative inferences that go beyond what was explicitly taught. |
| Organizing Students to Interact | The teacher organizes students to interact in a thoughtful way that facilitates collaboration. |

Context

Engagement

Noticing When Students Are Not Engaged and Reacting	The teacher notes which students are not engaged and takes overt action to re-engage those students.
Increasing Response Rates	The teacher maintains student engagement by using response-rate techniques during questioning.
Using Physical Movement	The teacher uses physical movement to keep students engaged.
Maintaining a Lively Pace	The teacher maintains student engagement by using pacing techniques.
Demonstrating Intensity and Enthusiasm	The teacher models intensity and enthusiasm for the content being taught.
Presenting Unusual Information	The teacher maintains student engagement by providing unusual or intriguing information about the content.
Using Friendly Controversy	The teacher maintains student engagement through the use of friendly controversy techniques.
Using Academic Games	The teacher uses inconsequential competition to maintain student engagement.
Providing Opportunities for Students to Talk About Themselves	The teacher provides students with opportunities to relate class content to their personal interests or lives.
Motivating and Inspiring Students	The teacher provides activities and resources that help students seek self-actualization and connection to causes that enhance the lives of others.

Rules and Procedures

| Establishing Rules and Procedures | The teacher ensures effective execution of rules and procedures through a process of review. |
| Organizing the Physical Layout of the Classroom | The teacher arranges his or her classroom so that it facilitates movement and a focus on learning. |

Demonstrating Withitness	The teacher displays *withitness* (or classroom awareness) to maintain adherence to rules and procedures.
Acknowledging Adherence to Rules and Procedures	The teacher consistently praises students or classes that follow the rules or procedures.
Acknowledging Lack of Adherence to Rules and Procedures	The teacher consistently applies consequences to students who fail to follow the rules or procedures.

Relationships

Using Verbal and Nonverbal Behaviors That Indicate Affection for Students	The teacher indicates affection for students through verbal and nonverbal cues.
Understanding Students' Backgrounds and Interests	The teacher produces a climate of acceptance and creates community by showing interest in students' hobbies and backgrounds.
Displaying Objectivity and Control	The teacher maintains objectivity and control in his or her dealings with students.

Communicating High Expectations

Demonstrating Value and Respect for Reluctant Learners	The teacher actively demonstrates value and respect for reluctant learners.
Asking In-Depth Questions of Reluctant Learners	The teacher actively engages reluctant learners in the classroom at the same rate as other students.
Probing Incorrect Answers With Reluctant Learners	The teacher treats the questioning responses of reluctant learners in the same manner that he or she does with other students.

References and Resources

Abrams, J. (2009). *Having hard conversations*. Thousand Oaks, CA: Corwin Press.

Achinstein, B. (2002). Conflict amid community: The micropolitics of teacher collaboration. *Teachers College Record, 104*(3), 421–455.

Ainsworth, L. (2003). *"Unwrapping" the standards: A simple process to make standards manageable*. Englewood, CO: Lead + Learn Press.

Anderson, L. W., & Krathwohl D. R. (Eds.). (2001). *A taxonomy for learning, teaching, and assessing: A revision of Bloom's taxonomy of educational objectives* (Complete ed.). New York: Longman.

Annenberg Institute for School Reform. (2004). *Professional learning communities: Professional development strategies that improve instruction*. Providence, RI: Brown University.

Aram, J. D., Morgan, C. P., & Esbeck, E. S. (1971). Relation of collaborative interpersonal relationships to individual satisfaction and organizational performance. *Administrative Science Quarterly, 16*(3), 289–297.

Argyris, C., & Schön, D. A. (1974). *Theory in practice: Increasing professional effectiveness*. San Francisco: Jossey-Bass.

Argyris, C., & Schön, D. A. (1978). *Organizational learning: A theory of action perspective*. Reading, MA: Addison-Wesley.

Bolam, R., McMahon, A., Stoll, L., Thomas, S., & Wallace, M. (with Greenwood, A., Hawkey, K., Ingram, M., Atkinson, A., & Smith, M.). (2005). *Creating and sustaining effective professional learning communities* (Research Report RR637). Bristol, UK: University of Bristol.

Brookfield, S. (1995). *Becoming a critically reflective teacher*. San Francisco: Jossey-Bass.

Bryk, A. S., & Schneider, B. (2002). *Trust in schools: A core resource for improvement*. New York: Sage Foundation.

Buffum, A., Mattos, M., & Weber, C. (2012). *Simplifying response to intervention: Four essential guiding principles*. Bloomington, IN: Solution Tree Press.

Chadwick, B. (1995). *Conflict to consensus workshop*. Minneapolis, MN: Minneapolis Public Schools.

Cherasaro, T. L., Reale, M. L., Haystead, M., & Marzano, R. J. (2015). *Instructional improvement cycle: A teacher's toolkit for collecting and analyzing data on instructional strategies* (REL 2015-080). Washington, DC: U.S. Department of Education, Institute of Education Sciences, National Center for Education Evaluation and Regional Assistance, Regional Education Laboratory Central.

Chokshi, S., & Fernandez, C. (2004). Challenges to importing Japanese lesson study: Concerns, misconceptions, and nuances. *Phi Delta Kappan, 85*(7), 520–525.

Coburn, C., & Russell, J. (2008). Getting the most out of professional learning communities and coaching: Promoting interactions that support instructional improvement. *Learning Policy Brief, 1*(3), 1–5.

Cochran-Smith, M., & Lytle, S. L. (Eds.). (1993). *Inside/outside: Teacher research and knowledge*. New York: Teachers College Press.

Cotton, K. (2003). *Principals and student achievement: What the research says.* Alexandria, VA: Association for Supervision and Curriculum Development.

Cuban, L. (1992). Managing dilemmas while building professional communities. *Educational Researcher, 21*(1), 4–11.

Darling-Hammond, L. (Ed.) (1994). *Professional development schools: Schools for developing a profession.* New York: Teachers College Press.

Darling-Hammond, L. (1997). *The right to learn: A blueprint for creating schools that work.* San Francisco: Jossey-Bass.

Darling-Hammond, L. (2010). *The flat world and education: How America's commitment to equity will determine our future.* New York: Teachers College Press.

Davey, L. (2013, October 1). 4 tips to overcome your conflict avoidance issue: Embrace productive confrontation. *Psychology Today.* Accessed at www.psychologytoday.com/blog/making-your-team-work/201310/4-tips-overcome -your-conflict-avoidance-issue on January 30, 2015.

Day, C., Sammons, P., Hopkins, D., Harris, A., Leithwood, K., Gu, Q., et al. (2009, June). *The impact of school leadership on pupil outcomes: Final report* (DCSF–RR168). London: Department for Children, Schools and Families.

Deci, E. L., Ryan, R. M., Gagné, M., Leone, D. R., Usunov, J., & Kornazheva, B. P. (2001). Need satisfaction, motivation, and well-being in the work organizations of a former Eastern Bloc country: A cross-cultural study of self-determination. *Personality and Social Psychology Bulletin, 27*(8), 930–942.

de Geus, A. (1988, March). Planning as learning. *Harvard Business Review,* 70–74.

Dirks, K. T. (1999). The effects of interpersonal trust on work group performance. *Journal of Applied Psychology, 84*(3), 445–455.

Donmoyer, R. (1985). Cognitive anthropology and research on effective principals. *Educational Administration Quarterly, 21*(2), 31–57.

DuFour, R. (2004, May). What is a "professional learning community"? *Educational Leadership, 61*(8), 6–11.

DuFour, R., DuFour, R., & Eaker, R. (2008). *Revisiting Professional Learning Communities at Work: New insights for improving schools.* Bloomington, IN: Solution Tree Press.

DuFour, R., DuFour, R., Eaker, R., & Karhanek, G. (2010). *Raising the bar and closing the gap: Whatever it takes.* Bloomington, IN: Solution Tree Press.

DuFour, R., DuFour, R., Eaker, R., & Many, T. (2010). *Learning by doing: A handbook for Professional Learning Communities at Work* (2nd ed.). Bloomington, IN: Solution Tree Press.

DuFour, R., & Eaker, R. (1998). *Professional Learning Communities at Work: Best practices for enhancing student achievement.* Bloomington, IN: Solution Tree Press.

DuFour, R., & Fullan, M. (2013). *Cultures built to last: Systemic PLCs at Work.* Bloomington, IN: Solution Tree Press.

DuFour, R., & Marzano, R. J. (2011). *Leaders of learning: How district, school, and classroom leaders improve student achievement.* Bloomington, IN: Solution Tree Press.

Eaker, R., DuFour, R., & DuFour, R. (2002). *Getting started: Reculturing schools to become professional learning communities.* Bloomington, IN: Solution Tree Press.

Elbousty, Y., & Bratt, K. (2010). Continuous inquiry meets continued critique: The professional learning community in practice and the resistance of (un)willing participants. *Academic Leadership, 8*(2), 1–5. Accessed at http://eric .ed.gov/?id=ED510036 on July 30, 2015.

Elmore, R. F. (2000). Building a new structure for school leadership. *American Educator, 23*(4), 6–13.

Eurich, T. (2013). *Bankable leadership: Happy people, bottom-line results, and the power to deliver both.* Austin, TX: Greenleaf Book Group Press.

Fairman, M., & McLean, L. (2003). *Enhancing leadership effectiveness: Strategies for enhancing and maintaining effective schools.* Dallas, TX: Organizational Health Diagnostic and Development.

Fernandez, C. (2002). Learning from Japanese approaches to professional development: The case of lesson study. *Journal of Teacher Education, 53*(5), 393–405.

Fernandez, C., & Chokshi, S. (2002). A practical guide to translating lesson study for a U.S. setting. *Phi Delta Kappan, 84*(2), 128–134.

Flora, S. R. (2000). Praise's magic reinforcement ratio: Five to one gets the job done. *The Behavior Analyst Today, 1,* 64–69.

Fullan, M. (2007). *The new meaning of educational change* (4th ed.). New York: Teachers College Press.

Fullan, M. (2008). *The six secrets of change: What the best leaders do to help their organizations survive and thrive.* San Francisco: Jossey-Bass.

Fulton, K., & Britton, T. (2011). *STEM teachers in professional learning communities: From good teachers to great teaching.* Washington, DC: National Commission on Teaching and America's Future.

Gallimore, R., Ermeling, B. A., Saunders, W. M., & Goldenberg, C. (2009). Moving the learning of teaching closer to practice: Teacher education implications of school-based inquiry teams. *The Elementary School Journal, 109*(5), 537–553.

Garmston, R. J., & Wellman, B. M. (2009). *The adaptive school: A sourcebook for developing collaborative groups* (2nd ed.). Norwood, MA: Christopher-Gordon.

Gottman, J. M. (1994). *Why marriages succeed or fail: And how you can make yours last.* New York: Simon & Schuster.

Graham, P., & Ferriter, W. M. (2010). *Building a Professional Learning Community at Work: A guide to the first year.* Bloomington, IN: Solution Tree Press.

Granovetter, M. S. (1973). The strength of weak ties. *American Journal of Sociology, 78*(6), 1360–1380.

Guskey, T. R. (2000). *Evaluating professional development.* Thousand Oaks, CA: Corwin Press.

Hallinger, P., & Heck, R. H. (1998). Exploring the principal's contribution to school effectiveness: 1980–1995. *School Effectiveness and School Improvement: An International Journal of Research, Policy and Practice, 9*(2), 157–191.

Hawley, W. D., & Valli, L. (1999). The essentials of effective professional development: A new consensus. In L. Darling-Hammond & G. Sykes (Eds.), *Teaching as the learning profession: Handbook of policy and practice* (pp. 127–150). San Francisco: Jossey-Bass.

Heflebower, T., Hoegh, J. K., & Warrick, P. (2014). *A school leader's guide to standards-based grading.* Bloomington, IN: Marzano Research.

Heifetz, R. A. (1994). *Leadership without easy answers.* Cambridge, MA: Belknap Press of Harvard University Press.

Herzberg, F. (1987). One more time: How do you motivate employees? *Harvard Business Review, 65*(5), 109–120.

Hoffman, P., Dahlman, A., & Zierdt, G. (2009). Professional learning communities in partnership: A 3-year journey of action and advocacy to bridge the achievement gap. *School–University Partnerships, 3*(1), 28–42.

Hord, S. M. (1986). A synthesis of research on organizational collaboration. *Educational Leadership, 43*(5), 22–26.

Hord, S. M. (1997). *Professional learning communities: Communities of continuous inquiry and improvement.* Austin, TX: Southwest Educational Development Laboratory.

Hord, S. M. (2009). Professional learning communities: Educators work together toward a shared purpose—Improved student learning. *Journal of Staff Development, 30*(1), 40–43.

Hord, S. M., & Sommers, W. A. (2008). *Leading professional learning communities: Voices from research and practice.* Thousand Oaks, CA: Corwin Press.

Hughes, T. A., & Kritsonis, W. A. (2007). Professional learning communities and the positive effects on student achievement: A national agenda for school improvement. *The Lamar University Electronic Journal of Student Research.* Accessed at www.allthingsplc.info/files/uploads/plcandthepositiveeffects.pdf on July 30, 2015.

Hutchins, E. (1990). The technology of team navigation. In J. Galegher, R. E. Kraut, & C. Egido (Eds.), *Intellectual teamwork: Social and technological foundations of cooperative work* (pp. 191–220). Hillsdale, NJ: Erlbaum.

Hutchins, E. (1991). Organizing work by adaptation. *Organization Science, 2*(1), 14–39.

Jackson, D., & Tasker, R. (n.d.). *Professional learning communities*. Cranfield, UK: National College for School Leadership.

Jaquith, A., & McLaughlin, M. (2010). A temporary, intermediary organization at the helm of regional education reform: Lessons from the Bay Area School Reform Collaborative. In A. Hargreaves, A. Lieberman, M. Fullan, & D. Hopkins (Eds.), *Second international handbook of educational change* (Vol. 1, pp. 85–103). New York: Springer.

Johnson, D. W., & Johnson, R. T. (2005). *Teaching students to be peacemakers* (4th ed.). Edina, MN: Interaction Book.

Johnson, D. W., & Johnson, R. T. (2007). *Creative controversy: Intellectual challenge in the classroom* (4th ed.). Edina, MN: Interaction Book.

Kern, L., White, G., & Gresham, F. M. (2007). Educating students with behavioral challenges. *Principal, 86*, 56–58.

Lee, H. (1960). *To kill a mockingbird*. New York: Grand Central.

Lee, M., Louis, K. S., & Anderson, S. (2012). Local education authorities and student learning: The effects of policies and practices. *School Effectiveness and School Improvement, 23*(2), 133–158.

Lee, V. E., Smith, J. B., & Croninger, R. G. (1995). Another look at high school restructuring: More evidence that it improves student achievement and more insight into why. *Issues in Restructuring Schools, 9*, 1–10.

Lee, V. E., Smith, J. B., & Croninger, R. G. (1997). How high school organization influences the equitable distribution of learning in mathematics and science. *Sociology of Education, 70*(2), 128–150.

Leithwood, K., Louis, K. S., Anderson, S., & Wahlstrom, K. (2004). *How leadership influences student learning*. Toronto, Canada: Center for Applied Research and Educational Improvement, Ontario Institute for Studies in Education.

Lencioni, P. (2002). *The five dysfunctions of a team: A leadership fable*. San Francisco: Jossey-Bass.

Levitt, B., & March, J. G. (1988). Organizational learning. *Annual Review of Sociology, 14*, 319–338.

Lewis, C. C. (1995). *Educating hearts and minds: Reflections on Japanese preschool and elementary education*. New York: Cambridge University Press.

Lewis, C. C. (2002a). Does lesson study have a future in the United States? *Nagoya Journal of Education and Human Development, 1*(1), 1–23.

Lewis, C. C. (2002b). *Lesson study: A handbook of teacher-led instructional change*. Philadelphia: Research for Better Schools.

Lewis, C. C., Perry, R., & Hurd, J. (2004, February). A deeper look at lesson study. *Educational Leadership, 61*(5), 18–22.

Lewis, C. C., & Tsuchida, I. (1998). A lesson is like a swiftly flowing river: Research lessons and the improvement of Japanese education. *American Educator, 22*(4), 12–17, 50–52.

Little, J. W. (1982). Norms of collegiality and experimentation: Workplace conditions of school success. *American Educational Research Journal, 19*(3), 325–340.

Losada, M., & Heaphy, E. (2004). The role of positivity and connectivity in the performance of business teams: A nonlinear dynamics model. *American Behavioral Scientist, 47*(6), 740–765.

Louis, K. S. (2006). Changing the culture of schools: Professional community, organizational learning and trust. *Journal of School Leadership, 16*(4), 477–489.

Louis, K. S., Kruse, S. D., & Associates (1995). *Professionalism and community: Perspectives on reforming urban schools*. Thousand Oaks, CA: Corwin Press.

Louis, K. S., & Marks, H. (1996). *Does professional community affect the classroom? Teachers' work and student experiences in restructuring schools*. Paper presented at the meeting of the American Educational Research Association, New York.

Louis, K. S., Marks, H. M., & Kruse, S. D. (1996). Teachers' professional community in restructuring schools. *American Educational Research Journal, 33*(4), 757–798.

Mackin, D. (2007). *The team-building tool kit* (2nd ed., updated and expanded). New York: AMACON.

Marzano, R. J. (1992). *A different kind of classroom: Teaching with dimensions of learning*. Alexandria, VA: Association for Supervision and Curriculum Development.

Marzano, R. J. (2003). *What works in schools: Translating research into action*. Alexandria, VA: Association for Supervision and Curriculum Development.

Marzano, R. J. (2006). *Classroom assessment and grading that work*. Alexandria, VA: Association for Supervision and Curriculum Development.

Marzano, R. J. (2007). *The art and science of teaching: A comprehensive framework for effective instruction*. Alexandria, VA: Association for Supervision and Curriculum Development.

Marzano, R. J. (2009). *Designing and teaching learning goals and objectives*. Bloomington, IN: Marzano Research.

Marzano, R. J. (2010). *Formative assessment and standards-based grading*. Bloomington, IN: Marzano Research.

Marzano, R. J. (with Boogren, T. H., Heflebower, T., Kanold-McIntyre, J., & Pickering, D. J.). (2012). *Becoming a reflective teacher*. Bloomington, IN: Marzano Research.

Marzano, R. J., Frontier, T., & Livingston, D. (2011). *Effective supervision: Supporting the art and science of teaching*. Alexandria, VA: Association for Supervision and Curriculum Development.

Marzano, R. J., & Heflebower, T. (2012). *Teaching and assessing 21st century skills*. Bloomington, IN: Marzano Research.

Marzano, R. J., & Kendall, J. S. (2007). *The new taxonomy of educational objectives* (2nd ed.). Thousand Oaks, CA: Corwin Press.

Marzano, R. J., & Kendall, J. S. (2008). *Designing and assessing educational objectives: Applying the new taxonomy*. Thousand Oaks, CA: Corwin Press.

Marzano, R. J., & Toth, M. D. (2013). *Teacher evaluation that makes a difference: A new model for teacher growth and student achievement*. Alexandria, VA: Association for Supervision and Curriculum Development.

Marzano, R. J., Warrick, P., & Simms, J. A. (with Livingston, D., Livingston, P., Pleis, F., Heflebower, T., Hoegh, J. K., & Magaña, S.). (2014). *A handbook for high reliability schools: The next step in school reform*. Bloomington, IN: Marzano Research.

Marzano, R. J., & Waters, T. (2009). *District leadership that works: Striking the right balance*. Bloomington, IN: Solution Tree Press.

Marzano, R. J., Waters, T., & McNulty, B. A. (2005). *School leadership that works: From research to results*. Alexandria, VA: Association for Supervision and Curriculum Development.

Marzano, R. J., & Yanoski, D. C. (with Paynter, D.). (2016). *Proficiency scales for the new science standards: A framework for science instruction and assessment*. Bloomington, IN: Marzano Research.

Marzano, R. J., Yanoski, D. C., Hoegh, J. K., & Simms, J. A. (with Heflebower, T., & Warrick, P.). (2013). *Using Common Core standards to enhance classroom instruction and assessment*. Bloomington, IN: Marzano Research.

Maxwell, J. (1995). *Developing the leaders around you: How to help others reach their full potential*. Nashville, TN: Nelson.

McLaughlin, M. W. (1993). What matters most in teachers' workplace context? In J. W. Little & M. W. McLaughlin (Eds.), *Teachers' work: Individuals, colleagues, and contexts* (pp. 79–103). New York: Teachers College Press.

Means, B., Padilla, C., & Gallagher, L. (2010). *Use of education data at the local level: From accountability to instructional improvement*. Washington, DC: U.S. Department of Education, Office of Planning, Evaluation, and Policy Development.

MetLife. (2009). *The MetLife survey of the American teacher: Collaborating for student success*. New York: Author.

MetLife. (2010). *The MetLife survey of the American teacher: Preparing students for college and careers*. New York: Author.

Mindich, D., & Lieberman, A. (2012, June). *Building a learning community: A tale of two schools* (Report). Stanford, CA: Stanford Center for Opportunity Policy in Education.

Morrissey, M. S. (2000). *Professional learning communities: An ongoing exploration.* Austin, TX: Southwest Educational Development Laboratory.

Moss, C. M., & Brookhart, S. M. (2009). *Advancing formative assessment in every classroom: A guide for instructional leaders.* Alexandria, VA: Association for Supervision and Curriculum Development.

National Center for Literacy Education. (2013, August). *Remodeling literacy learning: Making room for what works* (Report). Urbana, IL: Author. Accessed at www.literacyinlearningexchange.org/remodeling on July 30, 2015.

National Governors Association Center for Best Practices & Council of Chief State School Officers. (2010a). *Common Core State Standards for English language arts & literacy in history/social studies, science, and technical subjects.* Washington, DC: Authors.

National Governors Association Center for Best Practices & Council of Chief State School Officers. (2010b). *Common Core State Standards for mathematics.* Washington, DC: Authors.

Newmann, F. M., & Wehlage, G. G. (1995). *Successful school restructuring: A report to the public and educators.* Madison, WI: Center on Organization and Restructuring of Schools.

Nye, B., Konstantopoulos, S., & Hedges, L. V. (2004). How large are teacher effects? *Educational Evaluation and Policy Analysis, 26*(3), 237–257.

O'Neill, J., & Conzemius, A. (with Commodore, C., & Pulsfus, C.). (2006). *The power of SMART goals: Using goals to improve student learning.* Bloomington, IN: Solution Tree Press.

Opfer, V. D., & Pedder, D. (2011). Conceptualizing teacher professional learning. *Review of Educational Research, 81*(3), 376–407.

Organisation for Economic Co-operation and Development. (2010). *Education at a glance 2010: OECD indicators.* Paris: Author.

Patterson, K., Grenny, J., McMillan, R., & Switzler, A. (2002). *Crucial conversations: Tools for talking when stakes are high.* New York: McGraw-Hill Education.

Pfeffer, J., & Sutton, R. I. (2000). *The knowing-doing gap: How smart companies turn knowledge into action.* Boston: Harvard Business School Press.

Putnam, R. T., & Borko, H. (2000). What do new views of knowledge and thinking have to say about research on teacher learning? *Educational Researcher, 29*(1), 4–15.

Rath, T., & Clifton, D. O. (2009). *How full is your bucket?* (2nd ed.). New York: Gallup Press.

Reinke, W. M., Herman, K. C., & Stormont, M. (2013). Classroom-level positive behavior supports in schools implementing SW-PBIS: Identifying areas for enhancement. *Journal of Positive Behavior Interventions, 15*(1), 39–50.

Rogers, K., & Simms, J. A. (2015). *Teaching argumentation: Activities and games for the classroom.* Bloomington, IN: Marzano Research.

Rosenholtz, S. J. (1991). *Teachers' workplace: The social organization of schools.* New York: Teachers College Press.

Schön, D. A. (1983). *The reflective practitioner: How professionals think in action.* New York: Basic Books.

Schön, D. A. (1987). *Educating the reflective practitioner: Toward a new design for teaching and learning in the professions.* San Francisco: Jossey-Bass.

Servage, L. (2008). Critical and transformative practices in professional learning communities. *Teacher Education Quarterly, 35*(1), 63–77.

Servage, L. (2009). Who is the "professional" in a professional learning community? An exploration of teacher professionalism in collaborative professional development settings. *Canadian Journal of Education, 32*(1), 149–171.

Shrivastava, P. (1983). A typology of organizational learning systems. *Journal of Management Studies, 20*(1), 7–28.

Shulman, L. S. (2004). *The wisdom of practice: Essays on teaching, learning, and learning to teach.* San Francisco: Jossey-Bass.

Stenhouse, L. (1975). *Introduction to curriculum research and development.* London: Heinemann Educational.

Stiggins, R., Arter, J. A., Chappuis, J., & Chappuis, S. (2004). *Classroom assessment for student learning: Doing it right—using it well.* Portland, OR: Assessment Training Institute.

Stigler, J. W., & Hiebert, J. (1999). *The teaching gap: Best ideas from the world's teachers for improving education in the classroom.* New York: Free Press.

Stoll, L., Bolam, R., McMahon, A., Wallace, M., & Thomas, S. (2006). Professional learning communities: A review of the literature. *Journal of Educational Change, 7*(4), 221–258.

Timperley, H., Wilson, A., Barrar, H., & Fung, I. (2007). *Teacher professional learning and development: Best evidence synthesis iteration (BES).* Wellington, New Zealand: Ministry of Education.

Vescio, V., Ross, D., & Adams, A. (2008). A review of research on the impact of professional learning communities on teaching practice and student learning. *Teaching and Teacher Education: An International Journal of Research and Studies, 24*(1), 80–91.

Wallace Foundation. (2013). *The school principal as leader: Guiding schools to better teaching and learning.* New York: Author.

Webb, N. L. (2006). Identifying content for student achievement tests. In S. M. Downing & T. M. Haladyna (Eds.), *Handbook of test development* (pp. 155–180). Mahwah, NJ: Erlbaum.

Weeks, D. J., & Stepanek, J. (Eds.). (2001). Lesson study: Teachers learning together. *Northwest Teacher, 2*(2), 1–21.

Whitaker, T. (2002). *Dealing with difficult teachers* (2nd ed.). Larchmont, NY: Eye on Education.

Witziers, B., Bosker, R. J., & Kruger, M. L. (2003). Educational leadership and student achievement: The elusive search for an association. *Educational Administration Quarterly, 39*(3), 398–425.

Yoshida, M. (1999). *Lesson study: An ethnographic investigation of school-based teacher development in Japan* (Unpublished doctoral dissertation). University of Chicago, Chicago, IL.

Index

MARZANO Research

Transform teaching and learning through high-performing collaborative teams

 Signature PD Service

Collaborative Teams That Transform Schools
The Next Step in PLCs

The core of a professional learning community is the network of collaborative teams—the groups of teachers who work together to improve student learning. Collaborative teams have the potential to transform major aspects of teaching and learning. Learn how to transition from teachers who work in isolation to teachers who work in collaboration and from stakeholders who think in terms of *my* responsibility to stakeholders who think in terms of *our* responsibility.

Learning Outcomes

- Discover elements of curriculum work that provide focus for high-performing teams, such as identifying essential content, creating learning goals, and constructing proficiency scales.

- Learn how to accurately measure the progression of student mastery of the essential content through a collaborative lens, including common assessment development.

- Consider how to use assessment data for adjusting instruction to meet individual student needs.

- Understand how to effectively lead and support the PLC process.

Learn more!

marzanoresearch.com/OnsitePD
888.849.0851